Undefeated

Undefeated

SAMANTHA WALKER-ROBERTS

WITH SUNDAY TIMES BESTSELLING AUTHOR

ANN CUSACK

mB

MIRROR BOOKS

M
B

MIRROR BOOKS

1

Published in Great Britain and Ireland in 2025 by
Mirror Books, a Reach PLC business.

Photographic Acknowledgements: Alamy

www.mirrorbooks.co.uk
@TheMirrorBooks

Print ISBN 9781917439299
eBook ISBN 9781917439305

Editing and Production: Jo Sollis, Christine Costello, Mark
Westwood
Cover Design: Jonah Webb

Printed and bound in Great Britain by
CPI Group (UK) Ltd, Croydon, CR0 4YY

MIX
Paper | Supporting
responsible forestry
FSC
www.fsc.org
FSC® C013604

For my three beautiful children.
'I love you to the moon and back'

PROLOGUE

THE COUNCIL meeting hums with chatter and inflated self-importance, and I suddenly feel awkward and out of place. Small and colourless. Nothing more than a cardboard cut-out amongst all these high-flying, fast-talking professionals.

Damaged. Demoralised. Defeated.

As we take our seats, and a silence settles around me, I remind myself I am no longer 12 years old. I am not that little girl.

'So pretty. Bet all your friends are jealous. Don't cry. I'm not gonna hurt you.'

'And so firstly to the issue of expenditure, and the rigor with which we must address our overspend…'

The cabinet members, arranged in a semi-circle in front of me, nod and take notes as they bat back and forth with ideas to reduce millions and millions of pounds of debt. The numbers are so huge they sound meaningless, and perversely they hardly seem that bad to me. This council is dragged down by debt, and I know how that feels. I remember all too keenly being unable to lift my head from the pillow, paralysed by loss, anger and shame.

'Yeah, you can have a lift, as long as you do something for me.'

'And so, to the next item,' says the council leader, and my skin tingles with anticipation. 'The purchase of liquid fuels.'

My heart sinks. Another debate. Another decision. More mindless figures.

Children's shoes. A Bumbly Bee light. Kylie posters on the walls. A family home or a monster's lair? Or both.

'Just do as you're told. And make sure you're clean.'

He had laughed in my face at that; spittle landing in my eye, dribbling down my cheek, as *he* questioned *my* hygiene. That humiliation, heaped on top of all the others, almost broke me.

'And the next item' – this time I am sure it must be my turn – 'is sewage.'

The resolve fizzes out of me, like a beachball with a pin in it. How can sewage be more important than this? Yet it strikes me, that on some level, the two topics go hand in hand.

'Stop snivelling. I'm ringing my mates now, coming round to chill. Come on, smile.'

'Our last item is the proposal from Samantha Walker-Roberts for an inquiry into child sexual exploitation and safeguarding measures.'

My breathing is ragged. My cheeks burn. I feel everyone is looking at me, but most people don't even know who I am. Month after month, it's been voted down. Week after week, I've fought back. Day after day, I've held on to hope.

Gang raped. So many times, in so many ways, by so many men. I lose count. It becomes one long continuous scream. And not one of them even asks me my name.

Then suddenly, like a streak of sunshine from behind the biggest cloud, it's happening. It's my time.

'The vote is in favour, the inquiry will go ahead,' says the chairman, matter-of-factly. The meeting ends, the low chatter begins again, and I resist the urge to stand on my seat and cheer. Wave my hands in the air. Yell at the top of my lungs! Sob uncontrollably. Instead, I allow myself a small, tight smile as I button up my coat.

The physical injuries took years to heal. The damage in my head will be there forever.

But you will never defeat me.

1

SITTING ON the sofa with Granny Pat, her with a large mixing bowl, me with my dessert bowl, both filled with cornflakes, I was in my element. Both of us were glued to *The Lion King* on TV.

'Do you need more milk with your cereal?' she asked, with a friendly nudge.

'No,' I mumbled, my mouth full – and my heart, too. 'I'm okay thanks, Granny.'

The film was long, and I lost concentration as the plot meandered along. But I was happy simply to sit alongside Granny, her plump arm next to mine. She understood I didn't like cuddles, snuggles and invasions of space. Just being next to her was enough for me. Granny Pat looked like a cross between the comedian Dawn French and the actress Miriam Margolyes.

Her hair was neatly bobbed, her blue eyes shone with warmth, and her love for me was folded into every crease of her kind face. She exuded the perfect balance of indulgence and straight-talking, of affection and discipline. My head was lolling with tiredness way before the credits rolled, and Granny said briskly, 'Let's wash these bowls and get you into bed, young lady.'

Granny had a smart spare room with satin Damask curtains and a matching bedspread, all in cream. Sinking into the mattress, with my favourite Esmerelda doll on my pillow, I was soon sound asleep.

Granny was always awake before me, and early the next morning I heard the reassuring hum of the radio and the soft chinking of cups and plates as she prepared our breakfast.

'Sammy!' she called. 'Eggs and soldiers! And I've made some for Esmerelda as well.'

Granny was virtually housebound, so sleeping over, as a six-year-old, should have been a burden; a bore for a lively child who could not, according to everyone I met, sit still for a moment. But visiting Granny was, without question, the highlight of my week. Those sleepovers were better than going on holiday. Not that we did anything particularly exciting; she and I just enjoyed pottering aimlessly around her house and garden.

My step-grandfather was bed-bound, so I might sit with him whilst Granny spoon fed him or propped up his pillows. On Wednesdays, since I was rarely at school, my parents and I took Granny Pat out shopping. Every week, without fail, she bought a bakery loaf, a half pound of tongue or corned beef, and a freshly baked Victoria sponge.

Afterwards, we'd have sandwiches and delicious jammy cake back at her house. But it was the sleepovers I loved the most. Those evenings on the sofa, her with her big bowl, me with my small one, the TV turned up loud to drown out the crunching sound of our cornflakes.

Granny Pat was a murder mystery fan, and over the years, she introduced me to classic whodunnits like *Jonathan Creek*, *Poirot*, *Murder She Wrote* and *A Touch of Frost*. I didn't mind what we watched on telly; I just wished the time would slow down, or stop altogether, so that I didn't need to go home. Our family house was only 15 minutes away, but it felt so much further than that.

Some weekends, if Granny Pat was busy, I visited my maternal grandparents, Granny Annie and Grandad Frank. They were a typical, picturebook old couple in a life-size dolls' house. Granny's hair was set in a blue rinse, she had slightly-too-large sparkling white dentures, and immaculately matched red lipstick and fingernails. She was around 10 years older than Grandad Frank, who was small in stature but with a neat pot belly. He was almost bald, except for an unapologetic combover, which intrigued me as a child. I couldn't work out how one length of hair covered so much of his head. Grandad kept a comb, along with a hanky, in his top pocket at all times; an emergency kit for a windy day, and we had plenty of those in Oldham.

On Saturdays, Granny Annie liked a mooch around the market or a look around Wilkinsons. Grandad Frank would order a taxi to take us all into town, enjoying a chinwag with the driver along the way. Whilst Granny Annie was buying fruit and vegetables, me and Grandad would be tucking into a turkey and stuffing muffin from the van near the market. And later I was allowed to choose a bag of strawberry bonbons at the sweet stall. In the evening, my parents came to collect me and take me home. And that was the saddest part of the day.

With Granny Pat, too, the problems only came when it was time for me to go home. In fact, I *was* the problem at home. An only child, I lived with my parents, John and Karen, and my pet cats, in a traditional two-bedroomed council house on a large estate. We had a dark green suite in the living room, lots of dark mahogany wood, and a patterned, pub-style carpet.

In my bedroom, I had Groovy Chick wallpaper and a matching duvet. The airing cupboard was in my bedroom, and a couple of times a year, Dad made home-brew, which he left to mature in the warmth of the cupboard. At those times, a pungent, wheaty, smell leaked into my bedroom, not unlike the whiff of sweaty socks. Turning over in bed and pushing my face into the pillow, I longed to be back with Granny Pat or Granny Annie.

'Why can't I live there?' I asked. 'All the time?'

At home, I was always in trouble. Too bouncy, too loud, too talkative, too everything! Superficially, I had everything I needed. I was well fed and well dressed. Our home was warm and clean. I had weekly private swimming lessons and I played football. I even went to cheerleading classes for a while, before deciding they weren't for me. And yet, I didn't fit in at home. There was a chasm between me and my parents, an emotional void, like an open wound, which I felt keenly. The closeness I craved, the bond I imagined should exist, in particular between a mother and a daughter, simply wasn't there. As a small child, I was unable to articulate or even to imagine what that connection should look like, or how it might manifest. I only knew that it was missing and that there was an emotional Grand Canyon between us. The absence was an ache, a physical pain within me. How much of this was perceived and how much it existed, I cannot tell. But it matters nonetheless that I felt it and that it hurt.

Aged five, I was taken by my parents for a private assessment on my bad behaviour. Later that same year came Child and Adolescent Mental Health Services (CAMHS) appointments at the hospital, where play therapists waved puppets at me and spoke in silly voices. Afterwards, I was diagnosed with attention deficit hyperactivity disorder. (ADHD). I had no idea of the significance, I only felt, as the verdict was delivered, that it was my fault and that I had done something wrong. I was conscious I needed to grow out of it as quickly as I could, to please my parents and improve the mood at home.

The next time I visited Granny Pat, I announced: 'I'm sick with ADHD, Granny! The doctors said so.'

She pursed her lips.

'Well, I don't believe in labels for children. You're not ADHD. You're Sammy.'

She handed me a slice of cake and the matter was closed. I was not required to explain, or to modify, or to improve myself at Granny Pat's. She loved me just as I was.

At home, however, it was like I had an invisible chip implanted that activated the moment I walked through the door. I was forever misbehaving, backchatting my parents, bouncing up and down on the sofa, and talking loudly so nobody could hear the TV. At school I was constantly in trouble for interrupting, playing the fool and talking when the teacher talked. I touched stuff I wasn't supposed to, everything I touched seemed to break, and the things I broke could not be fixed. There was a long list of my misdemeanours, and every day, it grew longer still. Strangely, my behaviour was never a problem at Granny Pat's or at Granny Annie's.

'She's been good as gold,' they always said.

And I had been. Without even trying, I seemed to conduct myself impeccably there. Those suppers with Granny Pat, each with our bowl according to size, were amongst the rare moments of true happiness in my childhood. In the years to follow, when I was dragged down by heartache and hurt, I held that image in my mind like a colour postcard – and I treasured it.

2

WHEN I was eight, I spent some Saturdays playing with a little girl who lived at the far side of our estate. We had become friends through the local football club, though she had never played in the same team as me. Her house was a 10-minute walk away from mine, but it was along busy, close-knit streets with lots of children out playing. One Saturday afternoon, she and I were upstairs jumping on the beds to see who could go the highest.

'See that?' she shrieked, tucking in her legs and almost hitting the ceiling.

'Wow!' I gasped breathlessly.

I did a jump of my own and then said:

'I need a drink. I'm way too hot.'

Leaving her lying like a starfish on the bed, I ran downstairs to the kitchen, where her father was washing dishes. Her mum was always at work and rarely around. When I asked for a drink of juice, he lifted me up on to the worksurface and reached for a bottle of cordial in a cupboard behind my head.

And then, two things happened at once. He put the cordial down on the work surface with one hand, as his other hand shot between my legs, right up to my underwear. It was over so quickly, like a lizard flicking out a tongue.

'Here we go,' he said, filling a glass from the tap. 'Now, that's our little secret, Sammy, okay?'

He patted my head, conspiratorially, and lifted me down on to the floor tiles. In a daze, I went back upstairs with my drink, unsure what had just happened to me. And by the time I got home, I was questioning whether it had actually happened at all. It was *so* fleeting; illusory almost. Quite literally, I could have blinked and missed it.

But, I hadn't.

'Now, that's our little secret, Sammy, okay?'

For the next couple of weekends, I was stuck at home, watching from my window as endless grey rain spattered against the glass. On the third weekend, I went to stay with Granny Pat. I enjoyed our usual routines, our cereal suppers and our murder mystery marathons. But the shadow from that day, the memory of his hand, warm and slightly damp from washing dishes, was like a stone in my shoe, a constant and distressing niggle. And yet, resilient in the way that children are, and trusting in the integrity of adults, I did not hold him responsible. I thought it was no more his fault than anyone else's. And so, the following Saturday, when the sun finally came out again, I went off to visit my friend. I must have called round later than usual, because when her dad answered the door, he said:

'She's already gone out to play. She's with a girl from school, who lives just off the main road. I'm not sure you know her, Sammy.'

I hesitated. I didn't want to go inside on my own, but it was a long walk back home for my little legs.

'Come on,' he said, making the decision for me. 'Let's see if I can find a number for her friend's mum and I'll take you over there if she says it's okay.'

I followed him inside and, without question, up the stairs and on to the landing.

'In here,' he said, pushing open a bedroom door.

Perhaps I thought he kept his phone numbers in his bedroom. Perhaps I just did as he said because he was an adult and I was a small child. Perhaps I thought nothing at all. But as I stood by the end of the bed, he suddenly pushed me backwards and, in that second, the air around us changed. There was a malevolence, a charge, which I'd never experienced before. Even before he touched me, I was terrified, fear juddering through me like so many electric shocks. With the curtains open, and the sunshine streaming in as a bright witness, he pulled my underwear to the side and raped me.

'Our little secret,' he said again, patting my head as though I was an obedient puppy.

What frustrates me now is that I do not remember any pain at all. I cannot recall screaming, or shouting, or crying. It was over so quickly and yet it will never be over. I live it every day and it sits, like a nasty troll, in a dark corner of my mind. My next memory is of him walking with me to the house where my friend was playing, reminding me to be careful of the main road and to stay within the estate. When we arrived, he squeezed my shoulder and said with an avuncular smile:

'Play safely, Sammy.'

He behaved as though nothing at all was wrong. And so I persuaded myself that was probably the case. Back at home with my parents, I was completely numb. As I lay under my Groovy Chick duvet that night, my thoughts pinballed, each one smashing into the next. Before I could make sense of one idea, it had been shunted aside by another one. ADHD plus trauma was a toxic mix. I did not have the vocabulary or the confidence to confide in my parents, nor did I believe I had anything significant to confide. Besides, I did not have heart-to-hearts with my mother – she and I just didn't share that level of intimacy.

There might as well have been a physical divide between us, a barrier or a painted red line. *Do not cross!*

Perhaps our emotional distance had its roots in physical behaviour. Linked to my disorder, I didn't like cuddles or physical proximity of any sort. I was not the type of child who had bedtime stories snuggled up under the duvet, or who cuddled on the sofa watching movies. I didn't even like to be held if I'd fallen and hurt myself, or if someone had upset me at school.

Sometimes, if my mother and I were getting on well, she would trace circles with a finger on the back of my hand, or at the nape of my neck. But that was all. And maybe this palpable distance between us was echoed in the way we communicated. The boundaries of all kinds were clearly delineated, so even if I had wanted to tell someone about the rape, I could never have chosen my mother. Though I did not know the attacker was wrong, I sensed the act itself was wrong, but as a child I didn't know how to act on an instinct alone. All I knew for certain was that I did not like it. I didn't play with my friend ever again and nobody questioned why.

'Now, that's our little secret, Sammy, okay?'

Almost a year later, I made friends with an older girl from our estate, Millie, who took me under her wing a little. Always keen to push the boundaries, I was happy to tag along with someone from secondary school. My parents, reassured that Millie was older, nearly 13, allowed me more freedom when I was with her. I could go a little further afield and stay out a little longer, too. One day, Millie took me to the home of a boy who, at 14, was five years older than I was. Delighted to discover he played football, I asked if we could practise shooting in his back garden. He threw off his coat for one goalpost and I did the same for the second one.

'You're in goal,' he said, firing a ball straight at my face.

He might have been hoping to make me cry, but I was not the sort of child to give him the satisfaction, and I kicked the ball back at him as hard as I could. Millie, who did not even like fresh air, never mind playing football, quickly went home in a sulk. I was not especially shy or short of assurance around older kids, so I was perfectly happy there on my own. I felt I'd been in goal more than my fair share, but that was a minor complaint. When it clouded over, late afternoon, I picked up my jacket.

'I'd better go now. I have to be in for tea.'

As I reached the steps, he put a warning hand on my shoulder, and said:

'You can't go home until you suck this.'

I had no idea what he was talking about, but I was too small to stand up for myself as he pushed me, aggressively, down the side of the house. There was a narrow gap between his house and next door, and it was dark and secluded, smelling of moss and damp.

'Here,' he said, unzipping his trousers and pushing his penis towards me.

'Suck it!' he demanded.

He was older than me and much stronger and I had no way out. Squeezing my eyes tight, I did as he said, bending at an awkward angle against the brick wall. For a few seconds, I held it, almost suspended, in my mouth. But then he thrust it further and the tip touched the back of my tongue. Retching, I fell backwards into the wall, shouting out in disgust. With a look somewhere between relief and anger, he zipped his jeans back up and I took my chance to scramble up the steps and away.

The whole episode had lasted probably less than a minute. But I felt the imprint on my tongue as surely as if he had stamped upon it. Back at home, I cleaned and recleaned my teeth. I examined my tongue in the mirror, anxiously checking for damage and disfiguration. It was another odd, isolated episode – another secret – which I pushed deep into my subconscious, where it seethed and festered like an ulcer. And even on my happiest days, there was always a dark shadow that followed me around.

3

Later in 2003, Granny Annie died. I was heartbroken, and furious that I was not allowed to go to the funeral; too young, too naughty, too everything.

At the house afterwards, one of my great-aunts slipped a pound coin into my hand.

'For the shop,' she said kindly. 'Why don't you have a walk outside?'

She meant well, but I felt further ostracised, palmed off, as if nobody wanted me around.

'I loved Granny Annie so much!' I wanted to shout. 'Why can't I say goodbye to her? Why wasn't I at the church?'

But instead, I slunk out to the corner shop and plugged my grief with sweets and chocolate, a behaviour pattern that would plague me later in life. With Grandad Frank now elderly and living on his own, we moved to be closer to him. For many people, moving house is stressful, but I discovered I enjoyed it. My new room was a blank canvas, waiting for me to make an imprint. In my element, I spent hours picking out colour schemes and persuading my mother to order paint samples and material swatches. I settled on some fabric from Ikea, and she hemmed the pink-patterned curtains whilst I helped to paint the walls. I chose a pink rug, a neat coffee table, and my big treat was a new day bed. I loved my re-imagined bedroom, and more than that, I had discovered a talent and a passion for interior design. For other girls, a treat might be a little handbag or a new pair of shoes. For me, it was a colourful window blind or a bedside lamp. I made myself a sign:

'Samantha's Room. Private. Please knock.'

I loved having my own space. The memories of the attacks bubbled away below the surface, though I did not recognise them as such. In the no-nonsense approach of a nine-year-old, I categorised the two incidents as: The Man. The Boy. I could not have explained any further and nor did I want to. But, as is also typical of nine-year-olds, I didn't dwell on them either, and I could not be miserable for long. I was quite content as I helped my mother to sew a fancy cushion to match my new duvet; the perfect pillow for Esmerelda to sleep on. I was becoming expert at putting my trauma behind me, if only temporarily. I just wish, as an adult, I could do the same.

Living near Grandad was fun. Often on Friday evenings, he and I watched TV together, a fixed routine of *Granada News* followed by *Catchphrase*. When Granny was alive, she had cooked pea and ham soup and baked puddings. And for supper, she'd bring out an old Celebrations tub, filled with a selection of different biscuits. I always chose a rich tea finger to dip in her cup of tea. It was an art form I never quite mastered, to retrieve the biscuit before it fell apart, but she never minded. Grandad and I missed her so much. He was not a natural chef, and our usual Friday night fare was tripe from the market, eaten with celery or radish, dipped in salt.

For a snack, we might have crackers and banana milk. The meals were not to Granny's high culinary standards, but the love was there, and that was what counted. Though we lived near Grandad, I sometimes slept on a pull-out bed in his spare room. I preferred being at Grandad's to being at home. It was in many ways an unspoken relief that I no longer lived near to either of my abusers. The months rolled into years and there were no physical sightings and no danger of me bumping into them in the street or in the local shop. Yet they still skulked around at the back of my head, like burglars waiting for an opportunity to pounce.

After I started secondary school in September 2005, my behaviour deteriorated again. I was unable to articulate or acknowledge the submerged pain from the attacks, and instead it burst forth in geyser-like explosions of what must have looked, to everyone around me, like temper tantrums. In class, I was even more of a handful, my mind flitting from one subject to the next and inevitably landing me in more and more trouble.

'Miss, why are we in here? How long until break? What question are we doing? What page is it on? Can I get a drink of water? Can I go to the toilet? Can I, Miss?'

My concentration was so poor that I couldn't bear to sit for more than a few moments without being distracted. And now I needed distractions more than ever, because I could not – would not – allow myself to dwell for a single moment on the shadows of the past.

The Man. The Boy.

Pretty soon, I was spending most of my days standing in

the corridor in disgrace. And when the headteacher passed by, instead of raising his eyebrows in surprise at my disobedience, he simply asked, sadly:

'What is it this time, Samantha? What have you done today?'

Sometimes, I was sent to see him directly and made to stand outside his door instead, which was, if nothing else, a change of view. At home, I seemed to be at constant loggerheads with my parents. I was hyperactive, fidgeting, talking, bouncing and jumping.

'Sit still!' said my mother, despairingly. 'Be quiet.'

But I couldn't. Before I even realised my mouth was open, the words were falling from my lips, diving like lemmings over a cliff. I was argumentative, too, challenging everything from bedtimes to mealtimes to whether I should be allowed to repaint my room again. In frustration, I threw my things on the floor or against the wall. It frightened me that I didn't understand where my anger came from, less still how to manage it. I was out of my depth not only with the world around me but also, more terrifyingly, within myself. For a little girl, it was a lonely place to be.

My parents seemed at a loss, too. Occasionally, I was grounded, for an afternoon or a weekend perhaps. Or I might be sent to bed early. But there was no set routine of discipline or punishments. Paradoxically, though the boundaries between us were clear, the boundaries for my behaviour were both weak and flexible and I lived on shifting sands. Alone in my room, miserable and confused, I sought solace in my pet cats, and they seemed to be my only allies sometimes.

My favourite was an old cat called Megan, who I'd had since I was a baby. Then a family friend had come across a cardboard box in an alleyway, with three wet and frightened kittens inside. We adopted them all and I named them Sox, Spot and Piper. I loved having a cat curled up on my windowsill or asleep under my bed. Somehow, it calmed me, the sound of their purring dissolving my anger and untangling the barbed wire mess inside my head.

'I wish I was a cat,' I told Sox, stroking his soft fur. 'You have it so easy, you know that?'

Of course, he didn't reply, which was part of his appeal. Moments later, my mother called my name.

'Sammy! Downstairs now! I've just had your teacher on the phone!'

I wasn't naughty or difficult on purpose. There was no malice in my misbehaving. I just felt I didn't belong. Not even inside my own brain. And worse, I was becoming convinced it was my fault that I was different. My fault I had ADHD. My fault that The Man and The Boy had targeted me. At home, just as at school, I was lonely and isolated. There was nobody else like me, I was sure of that. But neither was I, by nature, a child who felt sorry for myself for long. Under siege, I used my loneliness as a weapon, as ammunition against the rest of the world. Being on my own, relying on myself, made me stronger. Or at least that was what I thought.

'I don't need you. I don't need anyone,' I told my parents. 'So there.'

And I marched out of the house with my head held high, as Megan watched from the window.

'See, I told them, didn't I?' I said, when she ran out into the street to sit with me on the wall. 'Me and you against the world, Megan.'

We were assigned a social worker, who came to the house to speak to us all.

'I want to go into care,' I told her. 'I don't belong here.'

As she peered at me in astonishment, my anger built steadily, like gathering storm clouds, threatening to burst. I didn't understand why I was so frustrated and why I felt so alone. And the social worker didn't understand either.

'Your behaviour is difficult and it's upsetting your parents,' she told me.

Clearly, *she* thought it was my fault too. At the end of the session, I ran upstairs and leaned over the banister, listening to them all as they discussed me in the hallway. They made a quip that I only wanted to go into care because I'd been watching the Tracey Beaker series on TV, which was about a girl in a children's home. Again, the fury surged through me. Why did nobody ever take me seriously? It might have been funny for them, but it was no joke to me. Over and over, I told them I was unhappy, and nobody ever asked me why. Sometimes, the social worker took me on outings: a walk around the lake, followed by a cake and a can of lemonade in the café.

'Now, Sammy,' she smiled. 'How about you try to behave better this week?'

But her buttery tones and bribes had little effect on me. Already, aged 11, my edges were hardened, and as I drained my lemonade, I retreated, slowly, like a wounded animal, back into the safety of my shell.

'Yeah maybe,' I said sullenly, kicking at the table leg.

Most of my friends from my early years had gone to different secondary schools. And in this new school, surrounded by cold and unfriendly cliques, my ADHD was just one of the challenges. I'd always been chubby, even as a small child. By the time I started at secondary school, I was a stone or so overweight. I had a daily £3 allowance to buy a healthy school dinner and pay any other expenses. But instead, I began spending the lot in the local shop, buying prawn cocktail crisps, choc-dips and penny mixes. Loaded up on junk food, I gained more weight, became upset about my appearance, and then ate more rubbish to make myself feel better about my situation. It was a vicious circle, one that many people can identify with. But it is also a very lonely place. And it became lonelier still when the other kids began taunting me and calling me names.

'Hey, fatso!' laughed a girl who I recognised from my class. 'Are you hungry? Because you could try eating this!'

She thrust a ball of old bubble gum under my nose, still glistening with spit, straight from her mouth. Though the tears pricked at the backs of my eyes, I lifted my chin boldly.

'Go on then,' I goaded. 'Make me!'

I was not especially worried by bullies. Even aged 11, I had a defiance and determination of spirit, strengthened by my role as outsider. Nobody fought for me. So I fought for myself. She crawled back under whatever stone she'd come from, and she never bothered me again. And, mostly, the other kids did the same. But behind my brave face, her words had hit a nerve, and at home that evening, I raided the cupboards for crisps and chocolate. Ripping open the packets and sighing with satisfaction as the sugar hit my bloodstream, I told myself I did not care. I reminded myself I had plenty of friends on the estate where I lived and that, anyway, I needed nobody. As I opened another wrapper, the carapace around me set harder still.

'It's you and me, Megan,' I said, licking chocolate off my fingers, as she purred under my bed. 'Just the two of us.'

In those first few months at secondary school, the MSN craze swept through my generation like a wildfire. Like most other kids around the world, I signed up, secretly thrilled at what it might offer. Me and my friends from the estate joined a website aimed specifically at teenagers and, through MSN, we competed to get the longest lists of the most online friends. It was a mark of status and popularity, and I was as eager as anyone else, while paradoxically swearing I was not swayed by approval or acceptance. The first question, before any conversation began, was 'ASL?' – age, sex, location. One afternoon after school, I logged on to see:

'15 – male – Wigan.'

'11 – female – Oldham.' I replied.

We chatted quite innocently online, but when my parents checked my account a few days later, they gave me a stern talking to. The social worker, in turn, gave me a lecture. His parents were furious also, and that was the end of our brief friendship.

'You're not to speak to any boys online,' my parents told me.

But if anything, getting into trouble had made me all the more determined to keep adding friends to my list. As was my way, I pitted myself against the adults in my life, and the website became as much about point-scoring against them as it was competing with my pals.

In December 2005, I turned 12, and my parents announced I could take a friend to the cinema to watch the new release of Narnia, so I invited my friend Millie. We didn't go to the cinema much, so I was excited.

I couldn't have admitted it, but I was so pleased that my parents were coming along too; that was the real treat. Though we were constantly arguing, I was, conversely, always in search of that elusive perfect bond I hoped we might one day share. I wanted to stay at home and feel that I belonged, equally as much as I wanted to be taken into foster care.

In the cinema foyer, we were allowed to choose whatever treats we liked and I picked out a big box of popcorn. As we took our seats in the darkened auditorium, I stumbled a little, spilling the popcorn everywhere, down the backs of the people in front, in their hair, and all over their seats.

'Sammy!' hissed an angry voice.

My heart plummeted. I had done it once again. I had landed myself in bother. Even on my birthday, I didn't seem able to behave myself. The Man was my fault. The Boy was my fault. The ADHD was my fault. And now this – my birthday was ruined.

'I'm not sorry,' I sulked, throwing myself into my seat, even though I was, desperately so.

'Sammy!' came the voice again.

As soon as I was old enough, I dropped the name 'Sammy'. I insisted on Sam or Samantha. For me, 'Sammy' conjured up harrowing memories of a childhood wrought with conflict and blame.

4

THE REPLY to the standard question flashed across my screen and I felt a shiver of excitement.

'18 – male – Stockport.'

18! He was an adult. A young man. Fumbling over the keyboard, I replied.

'13 – female – Oldham.'

It was only a small fib, and I felt 13 sounded so much more grown-up and mature. I couldn't wait to be a teenager. People were always telling me I looked older than I was, so it didn't seem too much of a lie.

'I'm Paul,' he wrote. 'Paul Waites.'

'Sammy Roberts,' I replied.

It seemed only polite to share my full name, as he had shared his.

'Have you had a good day, Sammy?' he asked.

'Not really,' I typed.

'Why?' he asked. 'What's wrong?'

'Nothing,' I replied. 'Honestly, it's fine.'

But he didn't leave it there. Paul kept on asking, kept on coaxing me, as though my problems really mattered to him.

'Tell me,' he wrote. 'Please. I might be able to help.'

'It's nothing.' I typed again.

I was in a bad mood. I didn't want to talk about my bad day at school, the hours spent standing in the corridor, the detention I had for tomorrow. In the end, he said:

'Look, I can't leave you all sad. I'm gonna try and cheer you up.'

Before I knew it, we were chatting away, and he was right: I started smiling despite myself.

'Favourite colour?'

'White.'

'Favourite animal?'

'Cat.'

'Favourite music?'

'R and B.'

There was no way a boy of my age would have been so patient and kind. And so interested in me. In fact, I couldn't remember a time someone had focused so completely on me, without it being to tell me off. Paul was really lovely. When it was time for me to go, he wrote:

'Same time tomorrow?'

'Course,' I replied.

I didn't need to think about it. I couldn't wait to talk to him again.

Our family computer was in a small room, like a pantry, just off the hallway, so there was some privacy. But then again, there was nothing to stop one of my parents poking a head around the doorway. After the way they'd reacted over the 15-year-old boy from Wigan, I didn't think they'd be too impressed by an 18-year-old from Stockport. Still, Paul was very polite and perfectly harmless. We chatted about the smallest of things, my history homework, my cats, my deliberation over whether to get my long hair cut shorter. Without even realising, I had found a friend, someone who cared, someone who really listened. And so to me, these were the biggest of things.

'I've never met anyone like you before,' I confessed.

'Me neither,' he wrote. 'You're special to me.'

His words sent a swish of excitement through me. Though he wanted to know all about me, Paul didn't seem interested in talking about himself much.

'I'd rather hear about you and your day,' he wrote.

I couldn't believe how nice he was. Considerate and thoughtful. Funny as well. Each day, I'd rush home from school, fling my coat and bag on to the hook and start up the computer before I'd even said hello to Megan. I couldn't wait to talk to Paul, just to share the details my day.

Got sent out of French – again. Teacher says she's going to have me suspended.

Bought a cheese wrap for dinner. Gross!

No decision on my hair yet…

We batted back and forth, quite innocently, a gentle game of online tennis.

'Show me your hair,' Paul wrote. 'Then I'll say if you should cut it.'

'How?' I asked.

He sent me his number.

'Send me a pic – can't wait!'

But I was suddenly nervous. What if he saw me and didn't

like me? The anonymity of the friendship, my true self obscured behind a keyboard, was the big appeal for me. I'd tried face-to-face interactions, and they just didn't work out too well. I wanted to keep it all online. But I wanted to make Paul happy, too. I couldn't bring myself to send a photo, but I did send him my number. I knew, of course, of the pitfalls of giving my number out to strangers, but Paul was not, by this stage, a stranger. He was a good friend. Besides, his email address matched his name: Paulgwaites@... And in my child's mind, that confirmed he was honest and trustworthy. He was exactly who he claimed to be. I'd got a mobile phone for my 12th birthday, but I'd not used it very much. I'd been too caught up with MSN on the computer. But I started texting Paul several times a day, just as I would any other of my friends.

Raining here

My cat looks sad

Have you had your tea yet?

He always, always, replied straight away, as if he'd been waiting for my message. And he invariably came up with something funny or kind, like he knew just what to say.

Then he began texting late at night, after I'd gone to bed, and I kept my phone under my pillow to muffle the sounds. Each time the screen flashed with his reply, a ripple of warmth ran through me.

'Thinking of you in bed,' he wrote. 'Miss you. Can't wait to talk again.'

'Me too,' I typed, aware I was beaming into the dark.

Sometimes, he'd message me on my way to school, too,

lighting up my bus journey with his funny comments or his concern. If he knew I'd had an argument with my parents, or a fall-out with one of my mates, he'd always check how I was. He never forgot.

Our chats became bookends; morning and night-time, starting and ending my day with a smile. And these were no longer inane exchanges about the weather or the latest cinema releases. Slowly, I confided in Paul about my problems; my fractured relationship with my parents, the feelings that I didn't belong, the belief that nobody wanted me around.

'I feel like nobody really gets me,' I told him, typing tentatively, knowing I was sharing a huge chunk of myself.

'I get you,' came the reply. 'You belong with me.'

My heart soared as I read his words. More than a friend, he was a confidante and an anchor, when I had previously felt weightless and untethered. I felt I could rely on Paul more than anyone else I knew. It was strange that we'd become so close, yet we'd never even met. Paul and I had been chatting for over three months when he said:

'I'm going to send you a photo. Hope you like it.'

The image that pinged up on my phone was not at all what I was expecting. Paul was naked from the waist up, his bare chest on show, with a moody stare behind sunglasses, directly into the camera. He had short, black dreadlocks with a colourful bandana around his head. He looked like a man. A real adult.

'Wow,' I breathed.

My phone bleeped again.

'Your turn,' he wrote. 'From the waist up. Naked. Show me everything.'

Reddening, I closed the message. I knew what he wanted but I didn't understand exactly why. I was a child, after all. In the distant recesses of my mind, a hazy connection was forming with The Boy: *'You can't leave until you suck this'* and The Man: *'Our little secret Sammy.'* Yet I could not join the link. Perhaps I didn't want to. So many different strands of thought whizzed around my head, splintered, disjointed and confused. I knew only that I felt sick, and frightened, and totally out of my depth. Just as I had back then.

'Can't,' I wrote. 'Sorry.'

I didn't want to let Paul down. I dreaded the thought of making him angry, or worse, disappointing him. But I couldn't send the photo. I just couldn't do it. After my message, I had second thoughts. I was worried I might have blown our friendship. But he couldn't have been nicer about it.

'Take your time. There's no pressure,' he wrote. 'I think you're really special. I wanna ask you something. Is that okay?'

'Yes,' I wrote, curious to know what was on his mind.

'Will you be my girlfriend?' he replied. 'I think about you all the time. I've never met anyone like you.'

My heart raced as I read and re-read his words, each one a small and shiny gem.

He wants to be my boyfriend! I've got a boyfriend! And not just any average lad from school. He's 18, he's tall, he's gorgeous, and he's mine!

The smile spread right through me, down my legs and arms, and tingling even in my fingers as I typed my reply.

'Yes! Course I will.'

I was walking on air, those next few days. It didn't matter about the bitchy girls in the lunch queue. The jibes just slid off me, like running water. It didn't matter that one day I was sent out of every single lesson.

I stood in the corridor, grinning as though I had just found hidden treasure. Which, in a way, I had. It didn't matter that I got soaked through on my way home from school and my socks were squelching in my shoes.

What was a bit of rain after all? Nothing mattered. Because *I* mattered. I mattered to Paul.

5

'LET'S MEET,' Paul suggested. 'I wanna see my girlfriend. Wanna see your smile.'

'Yes,' I replied. 'Definitely, yes!'

My stomach did somersaults of excitement. I couldn't wait.

'Let's do it tomorrow,' he wrote. 'In the afternoon maybe?'

My elation dissolved quickly into dismay.

'I'm at school,' I replied. 'Can't. Need to think about this.'

I couldn't just take the afternoon off. My teachers would notice. My parents would notice. I was in enough trouble every day as it was. Besides, I needed time to build up to meeting him. It was a big deal for me. But Paul, as always, was patient and understanding.

'Name the day,' he said. 'I'll be there. But keep it to yourself; I don't want you to get in trouble.'

'Okay,' I agreed. 'I'll sort it out as soon as I can.'

I wanna see my girlfriend… I think you're special… I think about you all the time…

I clasped his words close to me, kept them in my pocket, like a hidden pearl. I had a boyfriend; a boyfriend who was willing to do anything, go anywhere, just to see me.

I kept his photo on my phone, and I wrote his number,

without a corresponding name, in my fluffy pink diary. For anyone else, it was just a collection of random digits. They made sense only to me. This was my secret. My prize. No doubt my status at school would have shot straight up into the stratosphere if the bullies had known about Paul. My Paul. I could have silenced those nasty comments once and for all and they would be sick with jealousy. But that wasn't what this was about. It was about being liked and being loved. It was about being understood. And so I didn't tell a soul about Paul. I didn't boast or brag about my older boyfriend with his shades and his bandana. Not even a hint.

This was something for me, and only me.

The summer holidays arrived, which made it easier, in theory, for me to slip out and meet Paul. But something was holding me back. I was not nervous exactly, but definitely a little unsure. I was worried we might run out of things to say. Worried he might not like me face to face. Worried I might not like him.

And there was something else too. That faint, far-off clang of warning. The Man. The Boy. Now this. It was a small piece of grit, stirred into the smooth happiness of my days, suggesting all may not be as it seemed. But I couldn't work out why I felt like that. Paul was so trustworthy, so considerate, so kind. He wouldn't let me down. Not like they did.

'Can't wait see you,' he wrote. 'You are my one and only.'

His admission sent a frisson through me.

'Same for me,' I replied.

I always enjoyed the school holidays, but I seemed to skip

through the long days that summer. Millie, my friend, called round for me most mornings and we'd hang about around the estate, waiting for something exciting, which never happened. Despite the mind-numbing boredom of those endless afternoons, I didn't tell her anything about Paul. He was my secret. And the knowledge gave me a little lift inside, like designing a new bedroom, all over again. One day, Millie, who was now 15, said: 'Let's go to the sexual health clinic. I need some condoms.'

My eyes widened. In truth, I wasn't exactly sure what condoms were for, but I didn't want to admit that. We set off for the clinic, glad to have a purpose for the afternoon. But when we arrived outside, Millie frowned and said: 'I don't want to go in, Sam. What if I get into trouble?'

'I'll do it,' I offered immediately.

I wasn't too bothered about controversy; it had followed me around for most of my life. Anyway, what was the worst they could do? I was used to people telling me no and sending me away. I marched in, confident I looked older than 12, and asked politely but clearly for a packet of condoms.

'Name, address and date of birth please,' said the lady behind the counter, filling in a form.

I answered all her questions truthfully, it didn't occur to me to do otherwise. She grilled me on my use of condoms aged 12 and I told her I had a boyfriend. She didn't need to know that I had never even met him. Once outside, Millie slipped the condoms into her pocket and grinned.

'Thanks Sam,' she said.

A couple of weeks later, we made a return visit to the clinic and again, Millie asked me to go in on her behalf.

'You must be having a lot of sex to need so many condoms,' I commented, unsure even whether it was one per session or if they could be reused.

'Oh, I am,' she said coyly.

But on our way home, she unwrapped the packet and threw the condoms one by one up into the trees, until they caught on the ends of branches. Pale and flimsy, they looked like witches' fingers fluttering in the breeze. As Millie snagged the last one on to a branch, I decided perhaps she wasn't having so much sex after all.

'All gone,' she said, squashing the packet into a bin. 'We'll have to come back next week.'

But I didn't mind the trips to the sexual health clinic. It was a bit of mischief for me, a way of filling the time, and nothing more. And even though Millie was trusting me with the most intimate secrets in her life, I didn't mention Paul to her at all. That same week, my social worker called in and suggested we go for a walk.

'It's a nice day and we could chat whilst we stroll,' she said.

I hadn't intended to tell her about Paul.

'And I'm chatting to an 18-year-old boy online. I've got a boyfriend.' I found myself saying.

It was at once a relief and a shock to say it out loud. There was a risk, I knew, that she might tell my parents, or even the police. I had no idea, even, if I was breaking the law. Was I allowed to talk to an 18-year-old boy online? Was he allowed to talk to me? Maybe subconsciously this was what I wanted, for an adult to step in and make the decisions, that I was out of my depth, to tell me off and to put a halt to the inevitable direction of our online friendship. Perhaps I wanted her advice and her view on the situation. Or did I want to impress her, to show her in my own childish way that I was a grown-up, and to prove that I could manage quite well without her input? Maybe it was a mixture of everything. I was so muddled in my mind, I couldn't possibly have known. My social worker gave me a sidelong glance.

'It can be dangerous to talk to older boys online, Sammy. Think about that.'

We stopped at a kiosk, and she bought me an ice cream, which I interpreted as a direct bribe for more information.

'Are you being completely honest about this 18-year-old boy?' she asked. 'Because we know you don't always tell the truth.'

But I just shrugged. The shutters were already down. My mind was closed. And I ate my ice cream in silence. I had tried to tell her, and she didn't want to listen. Same old story.

6

AT THE end of August, just before the new school year began, Paul's messages took on a different tone. He became
more insistent and forceful, and behind the sugar-coated
words, I detected an urgency and a veiled ultimatum.

'I really wanna be with you,' he wrote. 'But I need to see
you. We have to meet, baby. I can't wait long.'

As I read his message, a shiver of panic ran through me.
I was worried I might lose him, that he might find another
girl who *was* willing to meet him – this very same afternoon.
Perhaps he had already found her. Perhaps he was with her
now? The thought made me sick with envy. I had rather
enjoyed holding Paul at a distance, admiring him from afar,
like a shooting star or a shiny bauble. But now, it was time
for action, and I could put it off no longer. Besides, if he was
really my boyfriend, my actual boyfriend – which was what I
wanted, wasn't it – then this was the next, natural step.

'Okay,' I agreed. 'I'll do it. I'll meet you.'

Briskly, Paul ran through my weekly timetable with me,
wanting details of where I was going to be and when. And
where my parents would be, too.

'Are there any times when you're out of the house on

your own without your parents?' he asked. 'Like at football training? Or cheerleading?'

'No,' I typed. 'Football's not on in the summer holidays.'

I'd given up cheerleading ages before that and I was a little hurt Paul had forgotten. He'd sworn he knew everything about me. But it was only a small mistake, so I didn't mention it. I racked my brains and then announced:

'But I have drum lessons! Every Thursday afternoon!'

'Perfect,' Paul replied. 'You can skip your drum lesson and meet me instead. I've got my own car. Send me the address.'

I enjoyed drum lessons and wouldn't normally have wanted to miss it, but my misgivings were swept aside by the revelation that Paul had his *own car*. I felt so mature, this was the adult way of doing things.

My boyfriend has a car! We're meeting up in secret on Thursday! He's going to pick me up and take me for a drive! I wanted to yell it from the bedroom window, which, conversely, was not the adult way at all. I did not see, aged 12, that Paul was sticking closely to my routine so as not to be found out. I just thought he was trying to be helpful and was going out of his way to make the meeting happen.

My drum lessons were with a Brazilian drum group, with members of all ages. I loved being in the band, and earlier in the summer, we'd paraded through Oldham, each with a drum around our neck, playing as we marched. My drum was hanging too low, and it bashed my shins every time I walked, so I had big bruises on my legs the next day. But I'd enjoyed the parade, nonetheless. The sessions were held in Oldham library in the town centre, so Paul arranged to meet me at Sainsbury's car park, which was opposite the library. He told me to set off for my drum lesson as usual, and even to go into the library carrying my drum bag and sticks, before doubling back to meet him. I was touched he'd thought it all through so carefully on my behalf.

'Delete all our messages – every single one,' he instructed. 'People won't understand, and I don't want you to get into trouble. I'm just looking after you, baby.'

As I deleted each wonderful message, my skin tingled with something in between excitement and dread. The innocent child in me loved the subterfuge; the idea that I was pitching myself against the adults in my life, that I was somehow getting one over on my parents. But no – *we* were pitching ourselves against the adults, *we* were getting one over on my parents. For it was me and Paul now. It was us. For the first time in my life, I had someone else on my side. Our meeting would be like an adventure, a clandestine treasure hunt, ending in the car park at Sainsbury's.

I loved the pretence of walking into the library, only to walk straight back out. Thrills ran through me like bubbles. Yet a part of me felt sickly and anxious too. This was not a game, I knew that much. It would begin with me missing my drum lesson. But how would it end? What was expected of me? Paul was an adult, with fancy sunglasses and his own car. Again, I had that sensation of being out of my depth. It was like paddling in the sea and the sand suddenly falling away beneath my feet.

Thursday afternoon came around more quickly than I would have liked, and my mind swirled with pitfalls and problems. What if the drum teacher called my parents to report my absence? It was unlikely, as there was a large group of us in the lesson, and it was the summer holidays, too, but still… And what if someone saw me with Paul? How would I explain it? It wasn't as if I had any other 18-year-old male friends. What if he didn't like me? Or worse, what if he liked me and wanted to kiss me? A cold fingertip of fear ran lightly down my spine at the thought. I was not normally a child who tormented myself like this, but I was plagued by one potential difficulty after another.

For an hour, I tried on different outfits in front of my bedroom mirror, discarding my leggings and my jeans and settling in the end for my favourite denim dungarees, which I wore with the bib down, and a plain, loose-fitting T-shirt. I wore my best FCUK jacket over the top. My entire wardrobe was still very juvenile and was possibly a little young for my age. I was an early developer and looked older than my years – everyone said so. But my choice of clothing was reflective of my mind and I was very much a child.

I didn't follow the trends of crop tops, short shorts and miniskirts like many girls my age. If I wore shorts, I made sure to have my leggings underneath. And my dungarees, baggy and comfy, were my favourite outfit. I didn't wear make-up, but once I was ready to leave, I smeared on a layer of my favourite strawberry lip gloss. And, as an afterthought, I popped into the bathroom to borrow a quick spritz of Mum's perfume. I stared at myself steadily in the bathroom mirror.

'This is it,' I said softly.

My parents had already offered to drive me into town for my drum lesson, but I'd refused, saying I was getting the bus early with some friends. The reality was, I still had told nobody, except my social worker, about Paul. He remained my secret, my sparkling gemstone. It didn't occur to me even to confide in a friend, for my own safety. Naive, as 12-year-olds are, I trusted Paul to be who he said he was, just as I was who I said I was. Much as I liked to pretend that I was immune to let-downs and deceptions, I wanted to believe what I was told. And to me, he was no stranger. We had been talking for nine months now. I thought he probably knew me better than most of my friends and family.

My heart was beating a little too quickly all the way there, and as I got off the bus at the library, my stomach lurched. This was the last place I wanted to be, yet perversely there was nowhere else I'd rather have been. As Paul had instructed, I followed my usual routine, as though I was being watched and monitored from a camera above. I didn't take one step out of line. I walked into the library, carrying my drum bag and sticks, exactly as I would have done prior to my lesson. But after a quick tour of the downstairs reception area, I checked my watch and left again, as casually as I could. What if he didn't show up after all this? My nerves were jangling so loudly, I wasn't sure whether that would be a good thing or not.

As I came out on to the walkway and into the afternoon light, I recognised, first of all, the bandana and the shades, it was Paul walking towards me. Here he was; he was real!

I could barely believe it. He half-raised a hand and smiled. Overawed, I blushed and smiled back.

'Hey,' he said, as we met on the walkway. 'My car's on the Sainsbury's car park. Shall we go and sit in there?'

I nodded and we turned together towards the back of the car park, the furthest point from the store entrance, where it was quiet. As we walked, I stole a sideways glance at him. In person, Paul looked quite a bit older than 18. Though at 12, I wasn't an expert on adults' ages. They all looked ancient to me, and I told myself I could be mistaken. Besides, everyone was always telling me how I looked older than 12. My friends had said I could pass for 16. There was nothing I could do about it. It wasn't as if I tried in any way to look older. And even if Paul was a couple of years older – I had lied about my own age, after all, by adding on a year – it surely didn't matter all *that* much. I reminded myself there had been a ten-year age gap between Granny Annie and Grandad Frank. That was perfectly acceptable, and they had been happy together for many years. So, by my child's logic, six or seven years between me and Paul was fine.

'Here,' he said, clicking his key and opening the door to a smart convertible sports car, silvery in colour.

'Wow!' I gasped. 'Is this actually yours?'

'Yeah,' he laughed. 'Get inside.'

I was impressed. I'd never been in a convertible car before.

'Can we put the roof down?' I asked.

'Maybe,' he said. 'Later.'

There was a beat of awkward silence, and I realised in a

rush how different it was, meeting in person. I wasn't sure I could think of anything else to say.

'I like your bandana,' I said eventually, in a small voice.

Even though we were inside the car, and it wasn't particularly sunny, Paul kept his sunglasses on, which made it difficult to gauge how he was feeling. I couldn't work out his expressions at all. But somehow, as my nerves settled, we got chatting and the mood between us relaxed.

'You're so pretty,' Paul told me softly. 'I'm glad you're mine.'

I shrugged self-consciously, but inwardly I was beaming.

'And I love this,' he said, reaching out to stroke my long hair on my shoulder.

He seemed to be staring right at me, but it was hard to tell, with the sunglasses. Then he pushed a button to move his seat back so that he was almost reclining, legs stretched. He was silent for a few moments, and I realised he was staring hard at his own crotch.

'What?' I asked, perplexed.

'Come on,' he said. 'Come on, baby.'

Again, he nodded towards his groin area, as though he was trying to show me something. I had no idea what.

'Come on, Sammy,' he coaxed.

But though his face was smiling, his voice was not. There was a steely undercurrent of impatience, annoyance even. Clutching my drum bag on my knee, I stuttered:

'I have to go now. My drum lesson would have been over ages ago. My dad will be wondering where I am.'

Paul didn't offer to drive me home and, as I stumbled out,

on to the car park, disorientated, I felt disappointment and relief in equal measure. Part of me wanted to stay longer. But a bigger part of me couldn't wait to get away. I ran to the bus station without once looking back.

'How was your drum lesson?' Dad asked, as I slipped off my shoes in the hallway.

'Yeah, good,' I replied, absent-mindedly, and I went straight to my room.

Lying on my bed, I suddenly, inexplicably, missed the smell of Dad's home brew and the malty whiff, which I'd once found so irritating, was now a familiarity, a comfort, which I yearned for. I thought of Granny Pat too, and wished I was on her sofa with my bowl of cereal. I longed to rewind, to unravel back in time. But I didn't understand why. Surely, I was on the cusp of something thrilling, I should be looking ahead, not behind me. And niggling, parallel to this, was the suspicion I had upset or angered Paul in some way. I worried I had let him down.

I'd never had a boyfriend before, and he was older and more experienced. He had a convertible car! That, in itself, epitomised perfectly the gap between us. Paul was worldly wise and sophisticated. Paul knew best, and I should listen to him. I was just a kid. The next time we met − if I was lucky enough to get a next time − I vowed I would not let him down. When I hadn't heard from him the next day, I began to feel a bit sick.

'Was nice to see you,' I texted.

No reply. I checked my phone every five minutes, as though it was burning a hole through my pockets. All day long, I fretted I had blown it.

'This is your fault,' I told myself. 'You should have stayed. Should have worked out what he wanted. You're to blame.'

By the following week, I was still checking my phone obsessively, logging into my account on the computer, desperately hoping for a message or a call. Paul was my best friend, and I missed him so much. I'd confided in him, trusted him, and he'd cut me off completely because of my own behaviour and my own stupidity. There was, I reminded myself, something wrong with me. I couldn't please my teachers, or my parents, or my social workers. I'd fallen foul of The Man. And The Boy. And now Paul. Nobody liked me. Why?

'What did I do wrong?' I texted.

I went back to school for the start of the new academic year, but my mind was elsewhere, and this time it was about so much more than an attention disorder. I couldn't go back to being a 12-year-old child. I'd crossed a line and there was no going back. I had an 18-year-old boyfriend, and my life was with him now. In lessons, I felt so far away, I might as well have been underwater. The sounds around me were muffled and distant and bore no relevance to me anyway.

'Samantha?'

The teacher's sharp voice cut through my daydreaming.

'Can you help us with an answer? It's basic algebra.'

I looked at her blankly. I wasn't even aware I was in a maths lesson.

In the next minute, I was outside in the corridor, adding my maths teacher to the list of people who didn't like me. As I leaned on the wall, waiting for the next bell, my thoughts jumped back over those conversations with Paul. How funny he was. How kind. How thoughtful. And he was gorgeous, too. The convertible car, the expensive shades, the cool bandana – he was any girl's dream. But what mattered most was that he had listened. He had cared. I'd been so lucky to have him. And now, I had lost him.

'You're a stupid kid, Sam,' I told myself. 'You blew it.'

That afternoon, I trudged home dispiritedly. The battery was dead on my mobile phone, so I plugged it in and lay back on my bed with Megan on my lap. As the phone charged, it suddenly bleeped, one, twice, and then again. Snatching it up, I read three consecutive messages from Paul.

'Baby, missed you so much.'

'Meet me this week.'

'Don't let me down.'

My fingers trembled with sheer relief as I typed my reply.

'Yes,' I replied. 'Yes, I'll be there!'

So pleased I'd been forgiven for my unspecified trans-gressions, I did not even question his lack of contact. His behaviour was classic child grooming, textbook coercion and control. But at 12, I knew nothing of that. I knew only that I was forgiven. I was back in the warmth of his sun.

'Thursday, same time, same place,' Paul wrote. 'Bring your drum kit, just like last time.'

'Yes!' I replied again.

'Remember, tell nobody.'

'No,' I agreed.

Overflowing with gratitude and appreciation, I would have agreed to anything.

'Delete our messages,' Paul reminded me. 'I don't want you to get into trouble. Remember, I'm just looking after you, baby.'

Thursday could not come quickly enough for me. The day before, I had a meeting with my social worker, who wanted to talk to me about my difficulties in school and at home.

'Your teachers say you're struggling to concentrate,' she said.

'That's right,' I replied.

'And there have been problems at home too?' she asked.

'That's right again,' I said.

My whole life was one big problem. But I didn't care any longer – because I had Paul. When she had exhausted the usual checklist, she began a lecture on the dangers of internet dating. The terminology made me feel quite grown-up and mature. I hadn't thought of it as 'dating'. That was a teenage thing. I was obviously more grown-up than I'd thought.

'Actually, he's not dangerous at all. In fact, you can meet him if you like,' I said. 'I've got a meeting set up with him.'

My social worker shook her head in a way that suggested she didn't believe a word I said. I told myself meeting Paul couldn't be such a big deal if she was so disinterested. Maybe girls my age did things like this all the time. She certainly didn't seem too concerned. That night, Paul called and asked me to switch on the webcam on my computer.

'I know I'm seeing you tomorrow,' he said. 'But I just can't wait until then. I miss you so much baby. Just lift your top for me, all the way up.'

My smile froze on my face.

'All the way?' I stuttered, my mood curdling. 'Why?'

Paul sighed. Just a small sigh, but it was enough to send a wave of worry through me.

'Do you want to meet me tomorrow?' he said.

And with that, with the threat dangling like a noose in front of me, I did as he said. I had to sit there for quite a while, naked from the waist up, and I was anxious one of my parents might walk past in the hallway. When I heard a footstep on the landing, I quickly pulled my top back down from over my head.

'Someone's coming,' I whispered.

He ended the call before I had even finished speaking. I felt grubby, and a little nauseous. But then later, I got a text.

'Baby, you are so beautiful.'

My heart swelled. This was what grown-up relationships were like. It was about doing things for Paul, even if I didn't want to. It was about taking the bad with the good.

After school the next day, I walked to the library with my secret carefully wrapped, like a delicate piece of jewellery. In the library foyer, I about-turned, and in that moment, I felt a wriggle of excitement. This was how it felt to be grown-up and in love. To have someone in my corner. To walk on the clouds. My parents could disapprove all they liked. Everyone around me could complain. But as long as I had Paul, my Paul, I didn't care. Still a little girl at heart, I loved watching Disney movies, the magical stories of *Cinderella*, *Beauty and the Beast* and *Sleeping Beauty*. Why couldn't I have my own fairytale ending too? It could happen for me in real life! *Happily ever after…*

Just the same as before, Paul was strolling down the walkway towards me, a bandana around his head. His sunglasses caught the sunlight, and for just a second, they glinted ominously, and my heart jumped. It was like that moment in a film when a baddie is introduced. Hurriedly, I pushed the thought from my mind. He wasn't a stranger, I knew him.

'Hey baby,' he smiled, quickening his pace towards his car, which I'd already spotted at the far side of the car park. We didn't speak until we were inside.

'I've really missed you, Sammy. You're gorgeous. I can't stop thinking about you. I wanna be with you all the time. I loved the webcam last night. You are so beautiful.'

Shyly, I smiled, his words running through me like warm honey.

'Me too,' I said.

'When you leave school, we're gonna be together,' he told me. 'Will you come and live with me? Be my forever girl? I can get us a place together. Don't worry about money or anything else. I'll look after you. What do you say? Will you be my forever girl?'

He took my hand in his and, blushing, I nodded. My heart was racing, I couldn't believe this was even happening to me. He had it all planned out. Always so unlucky, always in the bad books, I was plunged, suddenly, into a wonderful fairytale. This was real-life Cinderella, just as I'd dreamed. I remembered my Esmerelda doll, my favourite as a little girl. She'd found lasting happiness with her prince, and now it was going to happen for me too.

'Come here,' Paul said, pulling me across the console

towards him. I leaned over to him, my heart jittery as I realised we were going to kiss for the first time. I'd never kissed a boy before.

'Just relax,' he murmured, his breath, unexpectedly sour, as his lips fastened on to mine.

But to my alarm, I felt his hands moving across my breasts and snaking quickly down in between my legs. I clamped my knees together, clenching my thighs, but he forced his hand roughly in between.

'Relax!' Paul said again.

This time it was an order, not a suggestion. Instinctively, I pulled back, gulping in the air. Torn and confused, I wanted so much to please him. *I miss you. I wanna be with you. I think you're beautiful.* But I didn't like this. It didn't feel right. Paul sighed impatiently, but somehow managed to keep smiling. He was always smiling. It struck me for the first time that a smile can be so much more scary than a scowl. He reclined his chair a little, so that he was leaning back, just like the first time. And then he loosened his belt buckle exposing an inch of dark skin just above his underwear. The buckle was an intricate design, and, as my thoughts thrashed around my head, I wondered if I could ask him about the buckle, inquire where he had bought it, distract him somehow. But I was drowning, clutching at weak and useless reeds in the water, and I knew it.

'Come on, baby,' he said.

My heart fell. This again. I still didn't know what he wanted from me.

'Sammy!' he said, and it was almost a snap.

For the first time, he removed his sunglasses and looked

straight at me, his dark, beady eyes drilling through mine. A shudder ran through me.

'Put your shades back on, you're scaring me,' I said, trying for a jokey tone. But my voice was small and shaky.

Still smiling, Paul sat forward.

'Let's go for a drive. You and me. We need to get out of this car park.'

I checked my phone and began babbling.

'I'm sorry. It's not that I don't want to, I do, but I can't go for a drive. I haven't got time. Not today. My parents will wonder where I am. Sorry, I need to go.'

I was already opening the door, gathering my drum bag and my school bag. I wasn't sure how much I was worried about being late home, and how much I just needed to get away from Paul.

Clouded with confusion and regret, I had the feeling again that I had let him down badly. That I had somehow failed. And on the bus home, came the confirmation I'd been dreading.

'If you wanna be with me, you need to stop pissing me about. I'm not meeting you again if you do this every time.'

Tears streamed down my face as I stared out of the bus window and my phone bleeped insistently with more of his angry messages.

'Do you want me or not?'

'You are not who I thought you were.'

'Prick tease.'

'I'm sorry,' I typed. 'I'm sorry. I'm only 13, remember. It's all new to me. Please give me one more chance.'

He didn't reply, and I didn't blame him. I'd had two opportunities now to figure out what he wanted from me, and I'd fallen short both times. Like The Man. Like The Boy. Like everything else, I'd messed up. By the time I arrived home, the messages had stopped. And that felt even worse. I'd rather have been subjected to his anger than his cold silence. I didn't hear from Paul the next day, or over the weekend, and I started to feel physically ill with anxiety. I tried to call him, but he didn't pick up.

'Do you want to meet again on Thursday?' I typed. 'I can miss drums. I don't mind.'

No reply. I felt wretched. I'd had my fair share of heartache, aged 12. But this was like nothing else. I had shown myself to Paul, peeled back my outer skin and let him see the corners of my soul. For days, I thought of nothing else and no one else. School passed me by in a blur. Each night, I cried myself to sleep with my phone under my pillow. I had opened myself up to a man who had scooped me out and then thrown me away. The rejection was a visceral pain and I was winded by it. I had nobody to confide in, because the only person who knew about Paul was my social worker, and she had made it clear she didn't even believe me. Whatever heartache I was facing, I had to do it alone.

'Sam, you're an idiot,' I told myself angrily.

In frustration, I shook my phone, willing it to ring or ping me a message. But it stared back, silent and impassive.

'You're right, you are an idiot,' it seemed to say. 'Your fault. Not mine.'

The following week, I was in my bedroom playing with

Piper when my phone bleeped with a message. Always hoping it might be Paul, and always disappointed, I grabbed it quickly, regardless. As the words danced on the screen, a mirage forming before my eyes, it was like a dream come true.

'Meet me this Thursday, baby,' he wrote. 'Cannot live without you. My girl.'

I had a detention scheduled at school that Thursday, and my drum lesson had been postponed. But I didn't dare tell Paul that. Thrilled to hear from him, I'd have cancelled Christmas if it meant being allowed to see him again.

'I'll be on the webcam later,' he added. 'I need to see you baby. I can't wait.'

The thought of huddling inside our little pantry and taking my top off again filled me with alarm. But I reminded myself that, in relationships, it was important to please the other person. Paul had promised to find us a place to live and to pay for everything himself. The least I could do was take off my top. Even so, after it was over, I had a long shower, scrubbing at my skin and closing my eyes to blot out the memory.

'Can't wait for Thursday,' he texted as I got into bed.

'Me neither,' I typed.

The minutes and hours dragged and the day just couldn't come around quickly enough. At the final bell, avoiding the detention queue under the uncompromising gaze of the deputy head, I raced out of school and on to the bus. I was breathless by the time I got to the library.

'Baby,' Paul said simply, and my heart did a somersault.

Everything was heightened. His dazzling smile. His smooth walk. His silky voice. I felt like I'd stepped into another universe where everything was brighter, nicer, better. We got into the car, and he said:

'You know I love you. So much.'

I gasped. In my head, a whole choir began to sing: *Sam, he loves you! He loves you! He loves you!*

It was so loud, they might just have had my drum group playing in percussion.

He loves you!

Flushed with pleasure, I whispered, 'I love you, too.'

Paul lifted his sunglasses on to his head and looked at me with a piercing stare, which seemed not to match his words. I was struck by how small and hard his eyes were, and I wondered if that was why he wore his sunglasses so much.

'Sammy,' he whispered, so quietly it felt more like an out-breath.

There was a slight pause and only in years to come would I look back and see the sickening significance of this moment, as my world tilted and turned and changed forever. For in the next beat of my heart, Paul had unzipped his jeans and pulled out his penis. Bewildered, I wondered how he could move on so quickly and clumsily from his declaration of love.

'Here,' he said roughly, taking my hand and pulling it over to him. The feel of it under my skin was repellent, rubbery and squidgy. I was catapulted suddenly back to being six years old, rolling out playdough on Granny Pat's work surface. This was the same squishy texture. Yet it could not have been more different. The image of Granny Pat's face, juxtaposed with Paul's, felt so very wrong. A few minutes had passed when Paul grunted and pushed my hand away. Without speaking, he grabbed my hair and yanked my head towards him.

'No,' I stuttered, shaking my head even as he held it, his hands, warm and sweaty, above my ears.

He forced me straight down on to his penis, and the taste, like sour milk, hit the back of my throat and made me gag. I tried to protest, tried to pull back, but he had me in a tight grip.

With my eyes screwed shut, I wondered what punishment awaited me at school for skipping detention. Had they already called home? My parents might already be on the warpath. I hoped I would still be allowed to choose a DVD to watch on Saturday night. There was a film I really fancied but I'd forgotten the name of it. As is sometimes the way in times of great trauma, the human mind concentrates on the small things. Because the big things would have blown me to smithereens.

Paul grunted again and shoved my head aside, grabbing a cloth, which looked like a tea towel, from the storage pocket in the driver's door. He did not speak or even look at me as he wiped himself clean. Simultaneously, my stomach loosened, and my throat tightened, and I knew I was going to be sick.

I fell out of the car and hurried across the car park, stopping only to retch at the side of a pillar in the bus station. I wiped a sheen of sweat from my face and staggered on a little further. Later, I was amazed to discover I'd had the presence of mind to grab my schoolbag from his car and to get on the right bus headed for home.

I was in a daze, physically ill with shock. What had just happened? How had he jumped from saying he loved me to making me vomit? Of course, the two issues were necessarily connected, but I did not see that then. And I did not, at first, link the attack by Paul in any way with what had happened to me aged eight and nine.

Those incidents, The Man and The Boy, had been stark and horrific. But they had been isolated and self-contained, without promise or potential. Paul was different. I had trusted him and invested in him. I thought I had loved him. Worse still, I had thought he loved me. But he had shattered our friendship, like a precious glass vase dropped from a great height. He might just as well have broken every bone in my body too.

Though it had felt nice to say I had a boyfriend, if only to myself, I did not want sexual love. I was 12 years old. I did not even know what sex was. I was looking for love in its purest fairytale form, and there was absolutely nothing pure about Paul.

Nothing at all.

Sam, you're an idiot.

'Where have you been?' my mother called, as I arrived home. 'You'd better get yourself in here now. School called. You were supposed to be in detention. They said you didn't show up.'

Without replying, I ran upstairs and locked myself in the bathroom, scrubbing at my teeth, over and over, to clean away the taste. I brushed until my gums bled and my teeth ached. Yet each time I thought I'd got rid of it, I'd get an aftertaste of sour milk, and the whole horrible process had to begin again. Even as I squeezed out more toothpaste, I knew, on the most fundamental level, that I would never get rid of the attack.

The stains, like the smell of sour milk, would follow me forever.

7

AND STILL, incredibly, I longed to hear from Paul. Angry with myself, with my own dependency, I questioned why I was waiting for a message from a man who had upset and hurt me so much. I understood nothing, as a child, of trauma bonding, of child grooming and exploitation. He had got under my skin so expertly, tattooed himself on to me, that I could not simply shrug him off. I could not make that cut.

This awful attack, which should have ripped us apart, instead brought us closer together, in secrecy and in shame. He was the only one who knew about it and so he was the only one who could comfort me. The thought of losing him was unbearable, for much as I loathed him, I missed him too. But the days passed, and there was nothing from him. I didn't know whether he was angry that I had let him down in some way and the lack of contact was a punishment. Or if he was worried that *he* had crossed a line? I shivered as I remembered again the way he had yanked my head down into his groin. That, I knew with certainty, despite my naivety, was not okay. Or was he, and here I shrank with humiliation, simply bored with me and unimpressed with my 'performance' in the car.

'Just call me,' I said, shaking my phone in desperation. 'Just call.'

A part of me clung on to the hope that there might be some explanation for the attack, that perhaps he was overcome with remorse and might apologise. But what kind of explanation could there be? And even then, I sensed I was kidding myself. I realised that he had executed a well-rehearsed plan and there had been no hesitation, no second thoughts. I kept on reliving how he had gripped my hair and forced my head downwards, almost like he was operating a machine. I saw again the expert flick of the tea towel as he cleaned himself. He did not even think how I might get clean. Truth was, I would never feel clean again. My kind and gentle Paul, who would never hurt me, had been a monster in disguise. I felt so ashamed that I had trusted him and let him in. I was always making a mess of things, and this was another of my disasters.

Millie called round that weekend.

'What happened to you on Thursday? They read out your name on the detention list and you weren't there. Did you get a suspension?'

I shrugged vaguely. I couldn't even remember being called back to see the deputy head or what the punishment actually was. I had taken nothing in at school or at home in the days since Paul had forced himself on me. It was as though my mind had simply shut down and I had built an instant brick wall between me and the rest of the world – in particular anyone in authority. Besides, I couldn't be bothered with school any longer. The backchat and wisecracks seemed so juvenile and facile to me now. I was past standing in the corridor, and seeing the headmaster and repeating empty promises to do better. What was the point? I had aged 20 years in that Sainsbury's car park. Disillusioned and despairing, I felt too old for education and all of its pointless rules and futile attempts at discipline. I was done with the lot. And I felt they had been done with me long ago.

'So?' Millie pressed. 'Where were you on Thursday?'

I wavered. I needed to confide in somebody, and I was too ashamed and scared to speak to an adult. Besides, none of them ever listened.

'Promise you won't tell,' I whispered. 'I met someone on the teenage website. Something happened and I think I might be pregnant.'

'Really?' she whistled. 'God, I had no idea. Oh Sammy, you should have told me. You can't have a baby, you're only 12. You need to go to the clinic.'

'Yeah,' I mumbled. 'I think I do.'

On Monday, I found it surprisingly straightforward to get my registration mark in school then head straight out for the sexual health clinic. Nobody even challenged me as I marched across the school yard. Millie met me outside the clinic.

'I think I might be pregnant,' I told a nurse who took me into a side room.

Looking back at my 12-year-old self, the irony breaks my heart. Back then, I felt so mature and world-weary. I had an 18-year-old boyfriend, I was organising clandestine meetings in sports cars, I was playing truant and lying to everyone around me. I had a whole other secret life. Yet at the same time, I was so naive that I truly believed I might be pregnant from an oral rape. The nurse filled out a form, handed me a pregnancy test, and I called Millie into the toilets to help. I had no idea how to do a test and in my confusion, I persuaded Millie to provide the urine sample instead.

'I can't do it,' I whispered. 'I just can't pee in here.'

It was too much for me to take in. My thoughts, always racing because of my ADHD, were now at top speed, tearing down a mental motorway, veering dangerously out of the fast lane and back again as I struggled to maintain focus. Capturing a single strand of my thought process was like trying to nail a jelly to the wall. Impossible. I was unsure whether I was pregnant. I was unsure what Paul had done to me and whether it was illegal. But I was sure I could not cope with any of this. I'd managed the first part, getting myself to the clinic. But I couldn't see it through.

'Negative,' the nurse announced, though of course the result meant nothing to me.

We collected more condoms whilst we were there, just because it seemed like a good idea. Aged 12, I was picking up contraceptives in the same way that other kids bought sweets.

'I can't face going back into school,' I told Millie, as we chucked condoms up into the trees. 'I'm going to give it a miss today. Nobody cares anyway.'

Some kids I knew from my old estate often hung around the churchyard in the centre of Oldham instead of going to school. Turning up there at lunchtime, I found a cluster of teenagers, some older than me, sitting under a tree.

'I'm having a day off school,' I announced, throwing my bag down.

'Good for you, Sam,' grinned a girl I knew.

'Have you got any cash?' asked another. 'For booze? We're running low.'

I had my daily £3 allowance for school dinners, and so I nodded. A few minutes later, I was striding into a shop around the corner, insisting I was 18 years old as I picked out a bottle of White Ace cider.

'Where's your ID?' asked the assistant.

I stared back, affronted. How was it I was old enough to endure the attacks from Paul Waites, to attend the sexual health clinic, and to play truant, and yet I couldn't buy alcohol? It was a shock for someone to acknowledge that I was a child. Shrugging, I left and joined the others to wait for a sympathetic-looking customer to agree to buy alcohol for us. It didn't take as long as you might think, and we were soon proud owners of a two-litre bottle of White Ace for £3.29. With the others chipping in, I still had enough left for a chicken-bake pasty from the bakers. Back in the church-yard, passing the bottle around, I began to feel pleasantly fuzzy and giggly. With every mouthful of cider, the pain inside seemed to dilute and diminish; not washed away, but certainly fading. I heard myself laughing and joking and agreeing to meet everyone again the next day. Each time Paul's face flickered in my mind, I chased it away. I told myself I was over it. A bad thing had happened, but

I was better now. When someone offered me a cigarette, I accepted with a smile; my first time smoking. There was a first time for everything. As I was finding out.

'If you're coming back tomorrow, bring a change of clothes,' one of the girls told me. 'Wearing a school uniform, you're asking to get picked up.'

The warning code for police in the vicinity was 5-0. When the shout went up, that was the sign to ditch the booze and scatter.

'Okay,' I smiled, feeling worldly.

This was way better than being at school. My only regret was not doing it sooner. Arriving home that evening, my parents met me in the hallway and immediately noticed I was swaying slightly as I took off my shoes. Slurring my words, I tried to come up with an excuse for being drunk.

'School called. They said you've been absent all day,' mum told me. 'You're grounded. You can't carry on like this, Sammy.'

I mumbled a response and staggered up to bed. The next morning, remembering the advice, I packed jeans and a hoodie into my school bag and headed out of the door. After registration, I slipped easily out of school again and got changed in the toilets outside Oldham market. The cubicles were disgusting, filthy and smelly, with discoloured tiles and broken flushes. I pinched my nose and tried not to breathe in as I pulled my hoodie over my head. But once outside, in the fresh air, with a whole day to myself, it seemed worth it.

For a few hours, we hung around the shops, and I treated myself to a pasty and a bag of crisps. In the afternoon, we loitered outside the shop and persuaded someone to buy us a bottle of White Ace, then we went off to sit on some benches at the edge of the estate. I loved the numbness and nothingness that drunkenness brought with it. Like an undecorated bedroom, my mind was a blank space, a clean palate. For just a few moments at least, I was whitewashed of all darkness. I was free.

'Where have you been?' my mother demanded, when I staggered in later.

I muttered something and, just like the last time, went straight to bed. The next week followed a similar pattern. I managed the odd lesson at school, here and there. But mostly, I spent my days hanging around the town centre, the churchyard, or the estate, drinking enough cider so that the mental merry-go-round in my head would at least slow down to a manageable pace. My daily allowance was pooled with the others to spend on cigarettes and cider, with a sausage roll or a pasty for lunch if there was anything left over.

'Samantha, you're going to be expelled if you continue like this,' my teachers warned. 'Can't you see how foolish you're being? You're throwing your education away.'

But I didn't see how I could throw away something that had never been mine in the first place. I had never fitted in at school. One afternoon, I was due to attend a course called Transform, aimed at helping children to lose weight. I'd been previously and enjoyed the sessions. There were other kids like me there, overweight and uncomfortable with it, which made me feel a little less alone. The sessions were friendly and relaxed. We played basketball and football and learned a little about healthy eating. But on this particular afternoon, I'd missed school and arrived home from a couple of hours of drinking with my mates. I was half asleep on top of my duvet when my mother came home.

'Samantha! Wake up!' She demanded. 'You have your class in half an hour.'

She waved a sandwich under my nose, and, suddenly nauseous, I heaved. The cider, sloshing around my empty stomach, felt like a bad idea. Under instruction, I rinsed my face under the cold tap and cleaned my teeth.

'Honestly, what will people think?' she sighed.

It seemed to me her main concern was not the fact that I was drunk, aged 12, but that people would realise I was drunk, aged 12. The thought was so depressing, it just made me want to drink even more. My parents had no idea why my behaviour had spiralled so disastrously and I accept it must have been very confusing and challenging for them. But that chasm between us had been there ever since I was small and the time for confidences and sharing had long gone.

'I don't care what people think of me,' I retorted. 'I just wish I could be left alone.'

Perplexed, she and Dad tried keeping me at home as punishment for my drinking, but I just ignored them. Besides, much of the time I would abscond straight from school, so they couldn't stop me. They couldn't cut my daily allowance, as I'd have had no money for food or emergencies.

'Sam, what are we going to do with you?' they asked.

There were meetings with school and with social services, who teased promises out of me that we all knew I wouldn't keep. Once all the boxes were ticked on all the forms, I was allowed to leave the meeting and continue exactly as I had before. Just two weeks on from my final meeting with Paul, I was, almost daily, skipping school, drinking and smoking.

I had not heard from Paul, not even a text message. The rejection hurt so much, almost as much as the attack itself. Though I hated what he had done, I wanted him to love me still. My feelings made no sense to me, and the pain blazed through me, red and raw. And my only solution was to drink more. I told myself that White Ace was the answer and that I could drink myself back to happiness. But underneath my forced smiles and my drunken laughter, the trauma ate away at me like dry rot. On the surface, perhaps, I looked okay. I was beaming and laughing and pretending I was having the time of my life. But stand on that same surface for more than a minute and it would crumble, before falling away into nothing.

8

OCTOBER HALF-TERM arrived. It had been three weeks since I had last spoken to Paul, and three weeks since he had forced himself on me. I used alcohol to blot out these two issues, both equally painful. But in the same way I might put an Elastoplast on to a heavily bleeding wound, it was hopelessly ineffective.

Friday October 27 began like any other day. Early in the afternoon, I had arranged to see four or five friends, and my parents offered to drop me off outside JD Sports in the town centre, which was our usual meeting point. I got dressed into my favourite, all-purpose outfit of dungarees, grey T-shirt, FCUK jacket and white ballet pumps.

'Hey Sam,' smiled my friends, as I got out of the car.

For a while, we wandered without purpose, as kids do, meandering up and down the streets and in and out of shops. I went into a pet shop to admire the rabbits, and I deliberated over buying a new scratching post for my cats with my savings. But I decided it would be awkward to carry around all day. Next, we went into a newsagent, where I bought a can of Diet Coke. Then we went into a shoe shop, and I tried on various pairs of school shoes, since my own were starting to pinch my toes. I found a pair I liked, and decided I'd call Mum to see if she'd come back with me the following day to buy them. Patting my pockets for my mobile phone, I had a sudden memory of leaving it charging at the side of my bed.

'Never mind,' I sighed. 'I'll ask her when I get home.'

Mid-afternoon, we took up our usual position, outside the small shop near Tommyfield Market, to wait for someone to buy us alcohol. The older ones in the group had already been refused service, so we were again reliant on passers-by. Three weeks in, I was learning to spot the likely candidates before they even replied. Today, a stooped-over man, who probably looked a lot older than he was, agreed to buy us three two litre bottles of White Ace in return for a can of lager for himself.

'Deal,' I agreed, handing over our cash.

I was quite pleased with myself as we carried our contraband under our coats and into the churchyard. Again, there was that feeling of maturity and worldliness I'd had when I was arranging to meet Paul. Here I was, aged 12, casually walking around town with my own alcohol. I look back now and wish I could shake myself; shock myself into running the other way. Meeting Paul and buying cider were glaring red flags that my behaviour was younger – not older – than my years. I was more vulnerable and susceptible than I could possibly have known, yet the danger never entered my head.

As we spread our coats on the ground and sat down, I wondered what Paul was doing right now, if he had another girlfriend and if he liked her more than me. There was a little stab of pain as I thought of him and I took a gulp of cider quickly to help chase it away.

'I'm going to get leathered today,' I announced, tipping the bottle back into my mouth. 'I just feel like it.'

My friends laughed as I passed the bottle on. It was half-term and the mood amongst us was good. I was determined not to be the dark cloud and I thought drinking would help to hide my anxieties. We chatted for a while before nipping into the McDonald's to use the loos, hiding our bottles under a tree before we left. On our way back to the churchyard, I bought my usual chicken bake from the bakery.

'Shall we get some more White Ace?' I asked.

'Sam, slow down. We've loads left,' laughed my friend.

It had been a cold, clear day, but late afternoon, a smothering darkness fell quickly and cast an eerie hue around the churchyard. I shivered and stamped my feet. I'd grown cold, hanging around all afternoon. I rooted in my pockets for my MP3 player and realised it was missing.

'I've lost my MP3 player,' I announced in alarm. 'I had it earlier. It must be on the ground here somewhere.'

I dropped to my knees to search in the grass, but one of the lads started laughing and held something up in his hand.

'Give it back!' I said.

He threw it to one of the other boys, who threw it back and I felt my frustrations rising. They were only teasing, I knew. But I'd drunk more than usual today, more than ever before, and my patience was fraying at the edges.

'Give it back!' I demanded, but they laughed again.

Blowing out my cheeks, I walked off to have a few minutes

to myself. Hopefully, when I went back, they'd be tired of winding me up. Nearby, a man in his 20s called me over to ask for a light. He was slim with dark, spiky hair and was carrying an old umbrella.

'What's your name?' he asked, as his cigarette glowed red.

'Samantha,' called my friend's voice behind me. 'And she's 15 years old.'

Bashfully, I smiled, and instead of correcting the lie, I stared at my ballet pumps. We chatted for a while, as he asked why I wasn't at school and why I was drinking so much.

'Half-term,' I hiccupped, as if that explained everything.

For a few minutes, we stood in silence, and then he asked: 'Fancy a snog?'

Almost in the same moment, before I could think of a reply, he pulled me into him and began kissing me. At first, I didn't object, my reactions were dulled by cider. I tried not to think of Paul Waites and the way he had kissed me in his car. This man had bad breath too and I wondered if it was a problem for all men. We hadn't been kissing for long when his hands slithered inside my dungarees, over my breasts and down in between my legs. Staggering backwards with a combination of shock and alcohol, I wiped my mouth.

'No,' I said. 'Leave me alone.'

I stumbled away through the trees, tears leaking down my cheeks as I rejoined my friends.

'That bloke just groped me,' I stuttered. 'He put his hands in my underwear. Disgusting.'

The boys were still chucking my MP3 player around, but I no longer cared. The Man. The Boy. Paul. And now this.

What was it with men that they felt they could treat me just as they liked?

'Sammy, you should report him,' said one of my friends. 'That's gross. He can't just go around grabbing young girls. It's illegal.'

'Yes,' I agreed, a thin shaft of clarity breaking through my drunken haze. 'You're right. I should. And I will.'

The police station wasn't far and I set off with a sense of purpose. On my way, I spotted a phone box and inexplicably I had an overwhelming need to speak to Paul. He was 18. He was an adult. He would know what to do. I managed, in that moment, to somehow shift aside the fact that he was the last person I should turn to. Having been attacked by someone else, I was turning back to my abuser for help. It makes no sense to me now, but it made perfect sense then. Physically, Paul might have moved on. But mentally, he controlled me still and I was bonded to him by trauma and shame. Besides, who else could I ask? Tragically, I thought he was all I had. I knew Paul's number by heart and as it rang out, my mood lifted a little, as if I was already passing my problem on to someone else. Maybe he'd charge over to Oldham and come with me to the police station. Maybe he'd drive me away from danger in his fancy convertible car. I refused to follow the thought through, that Paul himself was the danger. He answered the call after a couple of rings, and just to hear his voice again was balm for my messed-up mind.

'I've been attacked,' I told him tearfully. 'A man in the churchyard assaulted me and I –'

'I can't help,' Paul interrupted. 'I'm busy.'

And the line went dead. I shook my head in disbelief as I listened to the disconnected tone. But I was, at the same time, weary and resigned. What else did I expect? As the phone box door slammed behind me, I realised I should never have called him at all.

You're stupid, Sam. You make the same dumb mistakes, over and over.

By the time I arrived outside the police station, the Debenhams store nearby was closing, so I realised it must be around 5.30pm. I was due home soon, and with that thought, I wished, more than anything, that I was back in my bedroom. Back with Megan purring on my knee as I watched a Disney film. Leaning on my bed cushions, flicking through colour schemes in my design magazines. Warm and safe.

Walking through the doors of the station, my nerves began to rattle. What if I was making a fuss about nothing? What if I got into trouble for drinking? What if I was to blame for pretending that I was 15? Perhaps this was all my fault, not the man's. I couldn't be sure. But then I remembered the way the man had pulled my T-shirt aside as his hands had grabbed at my skin. I had to tell someone. Near the front desk, a bald officer wearing a hi-vis jacket asked me what was wrong.

'I've been attacked just now in the churchyard,' I mumbled. 'I want to report an assault.'

He looked at me for a moment.

'Go home, sober up, and come back with an adult.'

Then he turned away, leaving me in no doubt that was the end of the conversation.

A little stunned, I made my way back outside. That was that, then. It was all my own fault after all. Even the copper thought so. My social worker had, more than once, accused me of making a fuss about nothing, and clearly that was the case again here. At the doors to the station, there were two men waiting. One man wore jeans with a jacket that had a white collar, and a second, darker jacket on top. The second man had a gap in his front teeth, and he wore a red jacket with dark trousers. The first man winked and beckoned me over with his index finger.

'Where are you going, pretty girl?' he asked.

I shrugged.

'Do you want to get in our car and chill for a bit?' he said.

He nodded over to the Register Office, where a dark-coloured car was parked.

'Okay,' I said listlessly, not really caring where I went or what I did. I was drunker than I had ever been and in the back of my mind, I knew I couldn't turn up at home in this state. I needed time to sober up. I was distressed by the sexual assault. Confused by the reaction of the police. Upset by Paul's indifference. Annoyed with my friends for pinching my MP3 player. I had nowhere else to go, so their suggestion seemed as good as any other. I walked with one man over to the car whilst the second went inside the police station.

'I won't be long,' he told us, explaining something about dropping his driving licence off at the front desk.

At the car, I got into the passenger seat and the man sat in the driver's seat. It was fully dark by now, but the streets were still busy with a blend of workers hurrying home and early Friday night revellers. Without even asking my name, the man said, 'Wank me off.'

He took my hand, and with my eyes closed, I did as he said. I was so taken aback by his bluntness, by the surreal situation, that I could not think of a reply. Halfway through, he released my hand and grabbed my head, pulling me on to his penis.

'No,' I protested. 'No!'

I flashed back to Paul Waites and that final horror inside his car. This was exactly what he had done, using my hand first before forcing me to use my mouth. Was I no good at it? Was that why both men had lost patience halfway through and changed tack? I'd fallen out of favour with them both, just as I did with everyone. Naturally, I thought of my parents. Maybe my tea was on the table, maybe they were wondering where I was. Again, I clung to the small thoughts, the minutiae, as I tried to block out what was happening to me. I retched as he pushed my head again and, in my mind, I pleaded for it to be over. But it seemed to last an age before the back door opened and the second man got in. There was no embarrassment or explanation, the driver simply fastened his jeans and started the car. I wiped my mouth with my sleeve, gagging on the taste, but not daring to say so. As we drove away, a voice from the back seat whispered.

'Feel me.'

His lips were touching my ear, and his breath was wet and warm. The realisation that I had fallen into a terrible trap hit me like a brick, and I wet myself out of pure terror. My knickers and dungarees were soaked, but to my relief, nobody commented. I was embarrassed. I couldn't remember ever wetting myself before. But I couldn't remember ever feeling this afraid. I thought they might kill me.

'Feel me,' he demanded.

Revolted, my mind screamed out against it and yet, I did not think I had any right to object. It seemed to me my opinions didn't matter. And what could I have done? I was a child, in a car with two adults. They had not so far been physically violent towards me, but the threat hung in the air as surely as if it was scrawled in blood across the windscreen. In any case, before I could formulate a reply, he grabbed my arm and pulled it round the back of the seat, pushing himself forwards so that I could reach his penis. My arm ached, it was uncomfortable and sore. But again, I dared not complain.

'Can we have sex in the back of the car?' he asked casually.

He might just as well have been asking if we could stop for a bag of chips.

'Can we?' he persisted.

'No,' I replied shakily. 'Please, no. I'm just a kid.'

He kept hold of my hand to pleasure himself as we drove around Oldham, some areas familiar to me, others not. At a crossroads, the traffic lights turned to red, and I realised if we turned left, we'd arrive eventually at Granny Pat's house. My mind was suddenly filled with images of our cereal bowls balanced on our knees as we laughed at Timon and Pumba in *The Lion King*.

How had I gone from that to this?

From the wholesome love and care of Granny Pat to the seedy depravity of these horrible creatures, whose names I didn't even know. The traffic lights changed, and we turned right. Probably just as well.

'Keep your hand here,' ordered the man from the back seat, yanking at my arm again. We drove around some more and then came to a stop outside a petrol station. One of the men got out and withdrew cash from a machine in the wall, and then we drove off. Soon after, we stopped outside a house. A man came out and cupped his hands to the window, peering at me like I was a fish in a tank. I had a terrible feeling he was weighing me up, as though I had a price ticket stuck to my forehead. He and the driver had a conversation in a language I didn't understand, before the man left.

'I need to go home,' I said, as we drove off again. 'Please.'

But they didn't seem to hear me at all. The driver swapped places with the man in the back seat, and their roles were reversed, one driving whilst the other assaulted me. I was expected to do exactly as they demanded. The houses and petrol stations slowly petered out and gave way to darkening fields and farmhouses as we found ourselves on the deserted moors, high above the town. My stomach lurched with dread. Were they going to kill me? Would they bury me here on Saddleworth, alongside those poor children who were murdered by Ian Brady and Myra Hindley? And how would anyone ever find me?

As we drove down desolate roads, in the pitch black, I hardly dared breathe. My whole body was stiff with morbid anticipation. I was so scared. Each time the car slowed, my heart raced, worrying we were about to stop. Worrying my life was about to be snuffed out. But then I saw the lights of the town coming closer, and realised we were driving back into Oldham. There seemed to have been no purpose to the drive around the moors except perhaps to frighten me. But even back in Oldham, I knew I was not safe in this car. I had to get out and I had to get home. I didn't know what to do. I was worried about angering them, but I needed to get away. I tried again:

'My parents will be worried. Please let me out. Anywhere is fine.'

I had no money for a bus, I wasn't sure if my bus pass would be accepted, and I didn't know what time it was or if the buses were still running. But I figured anything would be better than being trapped in this car. And what if they never let me out? What if they decided to kill me instead? I had seen their faces after all. I could describe them, pick them out in a line-up. Maybe they would silence me, for good. I had never, as a child, been confronted so brutally with my own mortality and I was trembling, from head to foot.

'Please,' I whimpered. 'Please.'

Still the men said nothing. We turned down a street with bushes on the right and garages on the left. A little further on there were some terraced houses. The driver pulled into the side of the road, and said:

'Off you go.'

His tone was pleasant, indulgent almost, as though he had done me a favour. I scrambled out quickly, overcome with relief, and realised I really had been expecting to die in there.

I felt so lucky just to be alive, and there was a moment of euphoria where the horror of the previous few hours quickly dissolved into the night air. But as I came to my senses, I was faced with another dilemma, for I found myself completely alone in a dark and unfamiliar place. As the car drove off, I noticed a lady coming out of one of the houses and I hurried over.

'Do you know the way to Fitton Hill please?' I asked. 'That's where I live. I need to get home.'

The lady had a kind face, but her English was broken, and she couldn't understand what I was saying. As we tried to make sense of each other, two men appeared from a different house, which had a black front door with wood at the window.

'Come in,' said one. 'I can help you.'

I hesitated, not wanting to go inside, but not having any other options. I had no idea how far from home I was. And the lady had disappeared back inside her house.

'Come on,' he said again, smiling.

I followed him, feeling, again, that I had no other choice. But inside, I spotted a pair of children's shoes in the hallway and felt immediately reassured. This was a family home, after all. Perhaps I could call a taxi, and my parents might pay the fare when I got home.

They would be furious, no doubt. But it seemed like the best idea. I allowed myself a glimpse, in my mind's eye, of my pink duvet on my day bed and of Megan curled up on my fluffy pink rug. How I wished I could close my eyes and magic myself there. Click my heels together like Dorothy returning to Kansas. Just thinking of the film made me intensely homesick.

From the hallway, I was shown into a living room with a blue carpet, a three-seater sofa, two single chairs and a portable TV. A girl, maybe not much older than me, was sitting on the sofa and one of the men went to sit next to her. He immediately began kissing her and groping her in front of me and, embarrassed, I looked away. The other man wore a white baseball cap, he had a gap in his teeth and bushy eyebrows.

'Can I ring a taxi please?' I asked. 'I need to get home.'

Even as I spoke, I sensed how pitiful and ridiculous that sounded. The front door was bolted. There was no way I was going home. Not yet. Maybe not ever. I had walked from one life-threatening trap straight into another.

Sam, you are so stupid. He's not going to let you go.

The man in the baseball cap seemed to read my thoughts because he laughed, a high, slightly manic laugh like a nervous teenage girl.

'Come on,' he said, grabbing my hand.

He led me upstairs on to a landing and I noticed he had a slight limp. I caught my breath, panic surging up my throat, as I spotted padlocks on all the doors except one. What sort of house was this?

'Is that the bathroom?' I asked, pointing to the only door that was slightly open. 'I need the toilet please.'

He nodded and I went inside. I wanted to clean myself up, after my accident in the taxi. But the taps didn't work, for some reason, and that seemed to upset me more than anything. How was I going to wash myself? How was I ever going to wash any of this off? Even then, I knew it was hopeless. Outside on the landing, the man opened a door and nudged me into a bedroom. There were purple curtains, a duvet cover patterned with purple squares, and a table at the side of the room. On the walls were posters of Kylie and Ashanti and some pictures of tigers. This was a child's room, I realised. Perhaps a young teenager. Someone around my age. The man leered at me, and I knew what he wanted. How could this be happening in a child's room with children's shoes in the hallway? I couldn't reconcile the two issues in my mind.

'I need to go home,' I whispered. 'Please let me go home. My parents will be worried.'

'Take your clothes off,' he said.

As with the two men in the car, he didn't seem to hear me. He didn't address at all what I had said and instead fired a demand at me. It was as though my voice was muted, or I was stuck behind an invisible, sound-proof screen. Nobody was interested in what I had to say. And when I didn't move, he pulled hard at my dungarees. I wore them with the bib down, so they came off easily, and my shorts underneath too.

'On the bed,' he ordered.

Recklessly, I thought of refusing, but I worried he might hit me, or worse.

He forced me to have oral sex, and as my mind whirled and twisted in protest, I wondered how this could be happening to me yet again. The man wore a ring on his finger, which caught my leg more than once and I felt the scratch. Resolutely, I focused on that scratch, on the mild discomfort, the slight sting, and I envisaged how it might look when I checked my leg later. Perhaps I'd need a dab of Savlon or a plaster. All through school, I had struggled to concentrate on one issue for very long, but now I closed my eyes tightly and zoomed in on the scratch on my leg. I imagined opening the bathroom cabinet at home, squeezing out the antiseptic cream and rubbing it into my leg. *All better now. See, it doesn't even hurt any more.*

When it was over, he put his jeans back on and then went to the desk to write something on a piece of tissue.

'My number,' he said, smiling through his crooked teeth.

Wordlessly, I took it and stuffed it in my pocket as I got dressed. I was just putting my jacket on when there was a knock at the front door.

'Put this on charge,' he said, handing me his phone and nodding to a plug socket. 'I'll get the door.'

My heart hammered as I waited in the bedroom, unsure whether or not I was allowed to leave. I heard some muffled conversation downstairs and then the man returned, pushing open the door and asking:

'How are you getting home?'

'I don't know,' I mumbled. 'But I will be okay. I just need to leave please.'

He rooted around in his pocket and handed me a jumble of coins.

'Oh, no, thank you,' I said hurriedly, unable to stop myself recoiling.

I didn't want kindness from anyone here. I didn't want to

owe him anything. In truth, I didn't even want to touch his filthy money. It didn't seem right in any way to take it. But then, none of this seemed right.

'Go on,' he said, pushing the coins into my hand.

He smiled, and against all my instincts, I heard myself thanking him. Thanking him for the pure horror I had just endured. Thanking him for the trauma, which I would relive over and over in my nightmares for the rest of my life.

'You're welcome,' he grinned, as though he found the irony hilarious.

He stood aside to let me past, and I ran down the blue stairs, stumbling out of the black door and away from that house into the cold, dry, merciless night.

9

I DIDN'T stop running until I reached the top of the street, which I recognised as a main road, and then I stopped, dizzy and breathless, to count the money. 84p. Not even a pound. It was a pitiful amount, a cold slap in the face, and encapsulated perfectly how I felt about myself. And probably how the man felt about me, too. This was what I was worth. My bus pass wasn't valid on all routes, so hopefully this was enough to pay my fare and get me home. But I didn't know where I was, or even if the buses were still running.

My mind, usually galloping along with a carousel of ideas, was blank and numb. Behind me, I heard a car engine, and I turned, hoping it might be a taxi. Could I persuade the driver to take me home and wait for payment whilst I woke my parents? They might be so angry that they wouldn't let me back in. I wasn't sure. But my heart lifted when I saw the taxi plate on the front of the car. It was a Nissan, blue or green, I couldn't tell in the dark. It slowed down and the passenger, a man in his late 20s or 30s, opened his window.

'Why are you crying?' he asked. 'What's the matter?'

'Nothing,' I sniffed, and I carried on walking.

The taxi kept pace, at the side of the kerb.

'We can help you,' said the driver, leaning over the passenger. He looked around the same age as the man next to him.

'It's too late for you to be walking around on your own. It's not safe.'

I stopped for a moment. My legs were tired. My whole body was tired. I no longer cared what kind of punishment awaited me at home. I just needed to be in my own bed with my cats purring on the windowsill and the memory of the smell of Dad's home brew itching my nose. Surely if I banged on the door and begged and pleaded, they'd forgive me?

'Will you take me home?' I asked cautiously. 'I don't have the full fare, but I can pay you when I get home. I've got 84p and my parents will have the rest of the money. Will you take me?'

'Course we will,' smiled the passenger.

He nodded towards the driver to prove his point and then got out to open the back door for me. As a little girl, I had been in so many taxis with Granny Annie and Grandad Frank. We always took a taxi for those Saturday trips to the market and back. The drivers were polite and respectful, and Grandad Frank liked to sit in the front and have a chat about the football results, whilst Granny and me sat in the back and wrote out our shopping list. Yes, taxi drivers were good people, I told myself. These men would take me safely home.

'What time is it?' I asked wearily, as I flopped on to the back seat.

'It's 11.15pm,' the driver replied, checking his phone. 'Far too late for you to be out. How old are you?'

'I'm 12,' I said.

'No!' he replied, laughing. 'No way you're 12.'

'I am,' I insisted, and for the first time that night, I half-smiled.

These men seemed nice and genuine. I had finally found someone to take me home.

'Fitton Hill please,' I said.

They didn't ask me for the name of the road, and we drove on further. A little while later, the car pulled up in an alleyway I didn't recognise. The driver got out and disappeared for a few moments. When he returned, he opened my car door and kissed me, full on the lips. Fear clutched at my heart; my skin shrinking around me in panic.

'Please,' I muttered. 'Not again.'

The man laughed.

'Am I going home?' I asked in a small voice, as he started the engine.

'We're going to my home,' he replied, and I saw him grin conspiratorially at his passenger.

We arrived in a more upmarket area, with bigger, new-build houses and cleaner, wider streets. He parked on a side road, with semi-detached houses in modern light-brown stone and grassed front gardens, on both sides.

'Here,' said the driver, offering me a cigarette as he opened my car door. 'This is for you.'

'Thank you,' I mumbled, aware I was once again thanking someone who did not deserve it, someone who was, I sensed, about to let me down in the worst way possible.

The hallway seemed long and on the left was a living room

with patterned curtains in orange, yellow and white. They did not, I noticed, match the blue carpet very well, and I stared around me as though I was here to redesign the place and to offer advice on colour schemes. I could not have admitted, even to myself, why I was really here. But in the pit of my stomach, in a whirling, frothing mass of terror, I knew exactly why I was here. It was going to happen again. Like some sick game of pass the parcel, I was being handed from one predator to the next, lurching from one abuser to another, like a commodity, a cheap asset. Who was in charge here? Who owned me? Not me, that much was clear. And where would this end? When would I be free? I didn't allow myself to answer that. Madly, I tried to focus on the carpet, wondering what colour would be better.

'Sit down,' the driver said, nodding at the sofa.

I did as he said, and again, I thought the sofa didn't blend too well with the rest of the room. With a flare of irritation, I questioned why I was concentrating on interior design. Why the denial? Why was I so stupid? It was going to happen. I had to face it.

Sam, you make a mess of everything…

Yet these two men seemed friendlier and more approachable than the ones from earlier. I wasn't sure whether this was a good thing or not. They chatted easily with each other, and then the driver disappeared into the kitchen and came out carrying a stack of plastic cups and a bottle of vodka with a red top.

'Would you like a drink?' he asked.

I shook my head.

'No, thank you,' I replied politely.

Even now, faced with the unthinkable, I remembered my manners. He pushed the vodka under my nose, but I shook my head a second time. My stomach was roiling as though I was out at sea. I was still drunk from the afternoon's cider, but at the same time I felt chillingly sober. I was starving with hunger, yet I could not have eaten a thing. The passenger from the taxi sat down, right next to me, so that his leg was pushing against mine. He was quite short, around 5'2" and he had a flat face. He told me he was 26 years old.

'I'm only 12 years old,' I repeated hopelessly, knowing it was futile.

For months, I'd fibbed about my age, telling Paul Waites I was 13. I couldn't wait to be a teenager, couldn't wait to fast-forward into the future. Now, all I wanted was to rewind. I longed to be six years old, sitting on the sofa with Granny Pat, with my cornflakes on my knee. My heart clattered against my ribs as I braced myself for what I knew was coming. Without even speaking, he pulled up my T-shirt and began to grab at my breasts with his right hand.

'They're gorgeous,' he said.

Inwardly, I was repulsed, but I did nothing. Like an animal, kicked to the gutter, time after time, I was almost out of fight. I had stepped into a nightmare, into someone else's hell, where every man I met treated me like a slab of meat.

'Let's go upstairs,' said the driver, interrupting the other man, and pulling me up by my hand.

Meekly, I followed. The driver was clean shaven but with stubbly eyebrows that met in the middle. He wore a dark blue fleece jumper, dark blue cord trousers and dark slip-on shoes. He was, he said, 27 years old.

'I'm 12,' I said again, my voice tight with desperation.

'Well, I'm 27,' he repeated, as though it was some sort of game.

He looked much older than that to me, but I reminded myself I was not good at guessing ages. I had thought the same about Paul Waites.

He pushed open a bedroom door and again, the disparity between place and purpose took my breath away. This bedroom belonged, without any doubt, to a small child. The yellow and green duvet, which should have been on the single bed, was piled onto a table at the side. There was also a heater over by the wall. On the tasselled lampshade was a picture of a bumblebee and the words: 'Bumbly Bee' underneath. I imagined a young child – the man's son or daughter perhaps – having a fixation, the way small children do, with a particular animal or insect. I envisaged them gleefully picking out the bumblebee lampshade and choosing the duvet to match. In my mind, I heard them sounding out the letters: 'Bumbly Bee' on the lampshade, as a mother or a father praised their efforts. Where was that child? Why was I in their room? Again, I could not let myself be led by these questions. The driver's voice snapped me back to a terrifying reality.

'Get undressed,' he ordered, his eyes roaming over me proprietarily, as though he was weighing up my worth.

He walked over to the table, opened a drawer, and got a condom out. I had a sudden memory of Millie and me, skipping down the street and laughing as we threw condoms into the trees. But I didn't feel like that scene belonged to me any more. It was almost as if it were a second-hand memory, and it had happened to someone else then described to me. I couldn't imagine ever feeling that light and carefree again, and I was unsure what was real and what wasn't. And why were there condoms in the drawer in a child's bedroom, of all places? Why was the duvet piled on to the table? It was as though the driver had been preparing for my arrival. As though he knew I would be coming here. But how? I was still standing there, fully clothed, after he'd ripped the condom packet open.

'Take your clothes off,' he said again, pulling his jeans down and throwing them on to the table on top of the duvet. 'Come on.'

'No,' I said in a small, stiff voice, which I barely recognised as my own.

He pulled at my dungarees impatiently, and I sensed he was becoming annoyed. Self-preservation kicked in and I reminded myself I was all alone in a room with a strange man. Bigger, stronger, and older than me. I didn't stand a chance. Shaking with fear, I did as I was told, removing the rest of my clothes myself. He pushed me back on to the bed and my whole body was taut. I was a rabbit in a trap.

'No,' I said again.

This time, I was pleading, begging. My eyes swam with tears. But he smiled and ignored me. He was still smiling as he raped me, stopping only to remove the condom part way through and flick it into a wastepaper bin. Afterwards, he continued the rape without any contraception at all.

'No,' I choked, my whole body shot through with pain. 'No.'

Four times I said no. Four times he ignored me.

'Put your ankles around my neck,' he ordered.

Petrified, I did as he said, and the agony ripped right through me. He might as well have sliced me open with a knife. It probably lasted minutes, but it felt like hours. Days even. And then, the passenger from the car was standing at the bedroom door, a harsh smile playing around his lips.

'You'd better be careful because we're both professionals,' he said to me, and the two men burst out laughing.

I didn't know what that meant, and though I tried to smile, to do what was expected of me, my face was frozen into a solid block. I felt like I'd never smile again. The driver stood up and I curled up on the bed, exposed and vulnerable and horribly aware of my nakedness. But I was too embarrassed to get up and find my clothes. The driver, meanwhile, was pulling on his own clothes, and he laid a hand, almost tenderly, on my thigh, before leaving the room.

'Okay, my turn,' the passenger said, as though I was a fairground ride or a board game. A free-for-all.

The rape began and he was forceful and cruel. Above my head, the Bumbly Bee lampshade swung gently back and forth, back and forth. I pictured the young child again, sounding out the letters as he sat up in his bed, cosy under his yellow and green duvet.

'B-u-m-b-l-y B-e-e'

In that moment, I wished I could be a bee too. Not only because I could fly away. But because I remembered watching a nature programme with Grandad Frank, which said bees lived for only a few weeks. Their lives were short, and at this moment, as my heart and soul were being pulverised, I no longer wanted to live. I wanted a short life too. When he had finished, the man said to me:

'Do you want me to get another mate round so we can chill?'

My mouth was swollen from him, my face was stinging where it felt like he had been biting me. My neck felt raw. I could not even process his words, less still make a reply. He remained in the bedroom, pawing at me and groping me, until there was a knock at the door downstairs. A few moments later, a third man came into the room and the passenger got up and left.

This was, I remembered, what had happened at the last house, and after the knock on the door, I had been allowed to leave. For a moment, I dared to hope the same might happen here. But then the third man began pulling off his black trousers and his white T-shirt.

'Lie back down,' he grunted.

My blood stilled and pooled in my veins as he climbed on top of me. I was raped again, and as it came to an end, I questioned physically how much my body could take and whether my only escape from this hell might actually be death. Like a poor little bumblebee, when I had served my purpose, I would simply curl up and die. The passenger was already waiting for the third man outside the room, and after he was finished with me, they announced they were leaving. I didn't speak. I wasn't sure I would ever speak again. The driver returned.

'Come with me. This bedroom is much more comfortable, there's a double bed.'

It was as though he was showing me around a hotel. His casual manner, his agreeable tone, jarred so violently with his abhorrent behaviour. Bent double with pain and shock, I followed him into a different bedroom. The double bed had towels, one green and one red, laid across the pillows and, on the mattress, there was a fluffy blanket or cover of some sort, with a religious symbol printed on it. Again, it was as though he had prepared in advance for my arrival. He knew I was coming, or if not me, then another young girl, another helpless victim.

'Get into bed,' he said.

Silently, I got in at one side, he at the other. I'd never shared a bed with anyone, let alone a complete stranger, and this was as bizarre as it was unsettling. He raped me again, asking:

'Do you like that? Do you like it when I go harder?'

'No,' I protested. 'No, it hurts.'

But he laughed as though I had given him just the answer he wanted, and he went harder still. I was so sore down below. And sorer still in my heart. When he had finished, he rolled over comfortably, as if to go to sleep. I lay there, rigid with anxiety, every pore of my body stretched wide with fear. I thought I was too afraid to sleep, yet incredibly, the shock and pain had exhausted me and I felt myself drifting off into a light, uneasy doze. When I woke up, with a sharp stab down below, he was raping me again. It happened over and over, a carousel of pure horror. Each time I fell asleep, I woke up to another attack, another sickening sucker punch. After each rape, he wiped me with a tissue and said:

'You have to be clean down below.'

It happened three times, maybe four. I lost count. And somewhere, in the clouded misery and fear, I lost myself. It was around 1.30am, according to the driver, when two more men arrived. He went downstairs to let them in.

'This is my room-mate and his friend,' he said, by way of introduction.

The room-mate wore black trousers and beige Timberland-style boots, though I noticed they were not Timberlands. Irritably, I wondered why I was again noticing such minor details, why I was more concerned with the trivial than the mind-blowing magnitude of the attacks. Yet how would it help me to focus on the rapes? I had no way out. I looked again at his clothes. He wore a dark jumper under a dark jacket and had spiky hair, which glistened with gel. He appeared to be in his late 20s, though he told me he was younger. His friend, who looked around the same age, was a medium build of around 5'7', with short hair and a clean-shaven face. Like all the other men, they were of Asian heritage.

'We're here to chill with you,' said one of the men. 'Okay?'

I knew better than to disagree, and uncertainly, I nodded. I understood exactly why they were here. They looked me up and down, as though, like the other men, making a valuation. I felt like a piece of furniture, or one of those poor lobsters in a tank in a fancy restaurant where the customer chooses their own dinner.

I'll have that one please… boil her up and serve her on a plate…

They chatted and laughed and pawed at me. But they didn't once ask my name. Nobody did, that whole night. My name didn't matter. And yet I wouldn't have wanted to tell them. They had stolen everything else from me, ripped away my dignity, my decency and my self-respect. I would not let them take my name and ruin that as well.

'Come on, back in the other bedroom,' said the driver.

Moments later, I was lying under the Bumbly Bee lampshade as the first newcomer raped me. I stared at the image of the bee as though he might rescue me from this. As though he might have a plan, where I did not. The pain was unbearable; it felt worse with every attack. I did not dare protest, in case I angered the man. But I could not help whimpering and crying. Staring at the lampshade, focusing on the bumblebee, I suddenly saw my own face staring back at me. I was no longer in the bed. I was no longer under attack.

Instead, I was hovering above it all, fluttering my wings like a little bee, watching the man thrusting uselessly into the mattress. I was free. Again, it ended. I had no idea how long it had lasted. Time seemed to have slowed to a standstill. I remembered those evenings with Granny Pat, how the time had flown and how I had wished they might last longer. Now, time seemed to shrink and stagnate. I was trapped here by the moment itself, frozen by the trauma.

The first newcomer finished, but the second one was already waiting by the bed.

'Kiss me,' ordered the second man, climbing naked on

top of me. Still floating, I watched from above as he began touching me and his hand lingered across my stomach.

'You have a big belly,' he laughed, and his friend laughed too, as he pulled on his trousers.

The words were like a body slam. Stunned, I fell from the safety of the lampshade, crashing on to the floor in a heap of shattered bones. Somehow, that single slight crushed me more than anything else, or at least I thought it did. I tried to pull my legs up, to hide my stomach, but he was already forcing me flat on my back so he could rape me. As it began again, his words ricocheted around my head.

You have a big belly. You have a big belly. You have a big belly.

From that night on, those words followed me and tormented me like school bullies, interrupting and destroying all moments of intimacy I ever had. With new partners, at the start of relationships, I heard again his voice and his cruel laugh, and I was awash with pain, as raw as it had been when he first said it. Even now, I insist on wearing a T-shirt during intimacy, because I cannot bear for anyone else to see my stomach. I don't even like to look at it myself, because I'm reminded of that man and his grotesque joke. It is one of the many, many, scars from that night.

When the rape was over, he sat on the edge of the bed, lacing his boots, and said to me:

'I recognise you, don't I, from the takeaway?'

I'd never heard of the takeaway he mentioned, and I'd never seen him before. His comments only added to my sensation of displacement, the belief that I had been dropped into a horror film, or into someone else's life. I was the wrong girl, in the wrong house, with the wrong people. That this should not and could not be happening to me. The two men left, and afterwards the driver took me back into the bedroom with the double bed. He raped me again in what, by now, felt like endless purgatorial pain.

Daylight was streaming in through the thin curtains, and I reckoned it was already breakfast time. My parents would be frantic. I had never stayed out all night before this. But then, I hadn't had any say in the matter. After the driver was finished with me, he said:

'You must wash yourself because I like cleanliness.'

Even aged 12, the stone-cold hypocrisy of his words smacked me full in the face and left me dumbfounded. It rings in my ears, even today. He pointed me into a poky bathroom and said:

'You need to shower. Sit on the toilet and pour the water from the sink between your legs.'

I didn't question these bizarre instructions and merely accepted a greenish brown towel from him to dry myself. I did as he had told me, desperate to sluice away as many of the physical reminders as I could. I did not think about the evidence I might be washing away, though that was clearly his plan. Afterwards, I went downstairs, and he patted the sofa next to him.

'Can I go home?' I asked timidly. 'Please?'

He patted the sofa again and as I sat down resignedly, he said:

'Once more.'

And he raped me on the sofa, the horrible jarring colours,

the orange, yellow and blue all bled into one polychromatic mess. The last drops of colour, together with the last drops of my childhood, drained away as I was raped for the final time. My world was grey, a soulless, murky, miserable grey. Again, he insisted I had to undergo his peculiar method of showering, promising he would take me home when I was clean. When he was satisfied with me, he said:

'Give me your number.'

My mind was too bruised and sore to think of a way out, and I mumbled my home phone number correctly. He took out his phone and typed in the digits and then he smiled at me and said.

'Now, you can go home.'

He said it as though I'd won a prize. Opening his front door, he added:

'Quick, get in the car. I don't want anyone to see you.'

You might have thought I would run for my life. Scream at the top of my voice. Smash the nearest window. But I was beaten and broken, and I could take no more. Like a zombie, I got into the car quickly and quietly, and he did too. We drove past landmarks that had previously been familiar and benign: the crematorium, the car wash, the park. They looked different now: sinister and threatening, and chained to the memory of the attacks. I hardly recognised these places I knew so well. Or maybe I was viewing them through different eyes.

It seemed years since I'd last travelled these roads. My old life was so far behind me, I could barely recall how it felt to have once been a child. To be 12. Ironically, I'd been trying to convince these men of my young age, and now, I no longer felt it. I didn't belong here, in Oldham. I didn't belong in this world at all.

'What time is it?' I asked him.

'10.30am,' he replied.

'What day is it?' I asked.

'Saturday,' he said.

I was blindsided. How could it be only one day? From the churchyard attack, at around 5pm, my whole ordeal had lasted around 18 hours. It felt like *18 years*. And yet each rape, each attack, seemed like it had lasted longer than all of the attacks combined. That made no sense. But none of this made sense. Time was looping back on itself, rewinding, fast-forwarding, stopping completely, until I had completely lost my bearings. Minutes and hours had become at once meaningless and vital. For in that 18-hour period, I had been raped and orally raped up to a dozen times by at least nine men. Like the minutes, the men all merged together in my mind, to form one terrifying behemoth.

Silence fell again and then, as we came within a half-mile or so of my home, the driver said:

'Is this your estate? You should get out here.'

'Thank you,' I muttered, cursing myself that, once again, I was thanking a monster for ripping my life to shreds.

I knew trouble would be waiting for me at home, and I could not bear the thought of it. Jingling in the pocket of my dungarees was the loose change the man had given me at the first house. I ran into a phone box to call Millie, hoping I could stay with her for a while, to delay the inevitable. But her line was engaged.

'Oh, Millie,' I groaned.

I spotted a postman on his round and crossed the street to ask him the time.

'10.45am,' he smiled.

Again, I was taken aback by the passage of time. It already felt like hours since the driver had dropped me off; the rapes had happened in a different zone, in a different world. Dazed and sore, I walked the rest of the way to Millie's house and collapsed into her hallway the moment she opened the front door.

'What's wrong, Sam?' she gasped. 'What's happened to your face? Mum! Come here!'

Her mother called mine and, moments later, she and my aunt arrived to collect me.

'Where have you been?' Mum asked. 'We've been worried sick. We called the police to report you missing. What were you doing all night?'

I didn't answer. I would not have known where to start.

10

I WAS silent on the short drive home. But the words built up inside me like I was a ball being pumped with too much air. I felt my lungs might explode with the pressure. The moment we got inside, I was bombarded by questions. I lifted my hands in front of my face, as if I could physically shield myself from the words.

'Where have you been? Who were you with? Why didn't you take your phone? You could have called. We've been out of our minds with worry.'

Dizzy and weak, I felt myself slipping further and further away, down a deep rabbit hole, until their voices were faint in the distance.

'Where were you?' my mother asked again.

Megan brushed against my leg and purred, and I looked into her big green eyes as though she might have the answers.

'I've been attacked,' I said quietly. 'I was forced to have sex. I need to be on my own.'

My limbs felt so heavy as I stood up and walked upstairs to my bedroom. Not long afterwards, there was a tap on my door and a police officer introduced herself.

'I'm trained in dealing with rape and sexual offences,' she

explained, perching on the end of my bed. 'I wondered if we could have a chat?'

I shrugged. Everything seemed meaningless. I had no burning desire to catch those responsible. I wasn't even sure whether they were at fault. Perhaps it was me. It was usually me.

'I'm not going downstairs,' I said. 'I can't face it.'

'That's fine,' she told me. 'We can talk in here if you like. But I have been told that you can tell lies. I need you to be honest with me. Can you do that?'

'Yes,' I said.

For a few moments, neither of us spoke. But the silence was pressing on me and crushing my skull and spine.

'I think I might be pregnant,' I said in a rush.

'What makes you say that?' she asked.

I shrugged again, unable to explain more.

'You don't think I am, do you?' I said.

It was both a challenge and a desperate plea.

'I really don't know,' she replied. 'But I can help you to find the answer.'

Again, the silence roared between my ears. I sucked in my breath and said:

'I might as well admit it. We were buying White Ace and drinking under-age. Am I going to get in trouble?'

'No,' she smiled. 'I can answer that one for you. You won't be in any trouble at all.'

More officers arrived and I was given a morning-after pill to take, as a precaution. I felt I had no say in the matter; I was swept along, a cog in a machine, a bit part in my own drama.

I knew these people were here to help me, but I felt that everyone was making decisions for me, just as the men had. I was not allowed to bath or wash or even clean my teeth. I had to hand over all my clothes, even my dungarees and my beloved FCUK jacket. As they were bagged up, ready for forensic testing, it looked like they were being thrown away into the rubbish, or donated to charity, as if I no longer needed them. As if I was dead. Which in a way, I was.

'Will I get them back soon?' I asked.

The officer pulled a face.

'Not soon, sorry,' he said. 'We'll need these for a while yet.'

Over his shoulder, I checked the list: 'Grey and white top, pink knickers, white bra, black and pink FCUK jacket, white top, black shorts, blue jeans, bus pass, 84p.'

84p. The shame, the disgrace, the self-loathing, was etched on the face of every coin. I wished I'd never accepted it. I wished I'd thrown it back in his face. Most of all, I wished I'd stayed at home. I was devastated to lose my clothes, especially my dungarees and jacket. They were mine; they were part of who I was. With each attack, with each rape, a small piece of me had been chipped away. Now I was losing my clothes, too. Soon there would be nothing left of me at all. Still on my bed, with my knees pulled up to my chest, I told the officer briefly what had happened to me, shame burning my cheeks as it went on and on, a never-ending nightmare of suffering.

'You're doing really well, Sam,' she said.

But she could not hide the shock from her face. At around 4pm, two new officers arrived to take me for a drive around Oldham.

'We want to try to find the houses where you were attacked,' they explained. 'We need as much evidence as we can get. Do you feel up to it?'

I shrugged. I didn't think my feelings mattered much either way. Besides, I didn't hold out much hope. I'd been drunk, scared and in unfamiliar areas in the pitch black. I had only patchy recollections of the journeys. I got into the police car outside, feeling, irrationally, that I had done something wrong.

'Just do your best,' said the female officer.

At first, everything seemed hazy. That first car journey, where we had driven round and round Oldham before moving out on the moors, was impossible to retrace. But I was more hopeful of finding the two houses. As we turned out on to the main road, we reached the traffic lights where I'd been picked up by the Nissan taxi, and I felt a sharp jolt of recognition.

'Here,' I gasped. 'This was where they offered me a lift, to take me home. This is where I met the driver and the passenger from the second house.'

Closing my eyes, I saw myself getting into the taxi. I spotted the covert smile between the two men. I heard my own voice, already, it seemed to me, infuriatingly naïve:

'Will you take me home? I'm 12 years old — I am!'

I had been a child when I last stood at these traffic lights. Now I was world-weary. Bruised, battered and broken. And old, so old. We drove on and I remembered clearly the section of Manchester Road that shared a junction with the road leading to the first house I was taken to.

'This is it,' I said. We're getting closer now.'

As we drew nearer, I spotted a green electric box, which jogged my memory.

'Yes!' I gulped, snatching at the air as though the oxygen was running out. 'This is definitely the right road.'

The street looked so ordinary and harmless in the daylight.

'There it is,' I said. 'The one with the wood across the window.'

It looked so different in the daytime, so ordinary. I could barely believe it was the same house. A tremor ran through me as I pictured the man in the baseball cap, his high-pitched laugh and the scratches from his ring. Inside the police car, I knew I was safe. But I did not feel it.

The officers noted the address, and we continued to drive. I was unsure of the route from the traffic lights to the second house. But then, I remembered the driver had stopped along the way. I was able to pinpoint the place and link it with the route that followed. As we turned into the street, I nodded. The houses, the gardens, the banality of the entire scene was filed, almost photographically, in my mind.

'That's the taxi,' I stuttered, pointing. 'That's the one, right there.'

Even as a child, I was stunned at the driver's blatant arrogance – or stupidity. Or maybe it was both. He had made little or no effort to cover his tracks. If it hadn't been for the car, I might not have been able to pick out the house itself. It was a generic new build on a cul-de-sac of identical houses. Each one had a square patch of grass at the front and there were no dividing fences or hedges to mark out one from the next. But the taxi, sitting smugly on the path, was a clear signpost. It was almost too easy, too convenient. Perhaps the men thought I'd never have the confidence to report them. Maybe they thought they were above the law, and they could treat young girls exactly as they wanted to. They seemed happy to give up the evidence. With two addresses and one car identified, the officers seemed pleased.

'Can I go home now?' I asked. 'I'm so tired. I've not slept.'

But next, I was taken to the rape crisis suite in Manchester, where I had to give a urine sample and a blood test, and provide several swabs.

'Do you want the numbing cream for the blood test?' asked a nurse.

Nervously, I nodded. I was worried about having a needle in my arm. But even with the cream, I felt a small scratch, and then to my alarm, the blood spurted everywhere.

'Oh dear, it looks as though we nicked a nerve,' said the nurse, throwing paper towels on to the floor. 'Not to worry.'

But my blood all over the floor looked sacrificial. I was being made to suffer and, I reminded myself, I deserved it. I'd got myself into this awful mess.

After the blood test, I had to be fully examined. Undressing for yet another stranger was mortifying. I was poked and prodded like I was an animal going to the abattoir. I could not help thinking of the attacks – one man after another forcing himself upon me. The circumstances were different here. But I felt equally exposed and under siege. And with each swab, with each sample, another part of me was whittled away. Would I ever get it back? I wasn't even sure I wanted my old self back. Later, the medical report would confirm that there were several types of semen found on me and on my clothes. The examination recorded an abrasion to my right breast, scratches on my arms, abdomen and left leg, bruises on my neck and my nose, and a piece out of my chin.

There was also an anal tear.

'You're doing very well, Samantha,' the officers told me. 'But now we need to speak to you at the police station, to formally record everything you've told us.'

I understood it was best to do the interviews whilst everything was fresh in my mind. But I was exhausted, physically crumbling after a night without sleep and so much stress. Besides, I did not feel I would ever forget the details of what I had been through. They would be as raw on my 90th birthday as they were now. My parents drove me to Oldham Police Station, and in the back of the car I felt as though I was fading into the upholstery, dissolving into the seat covers. I was becoming a hologram of my old self. Only the presence of my parents, solid and real, gave me context for who I was and why I was here. Outside, the October rain streaked the windows like tears.

The police interview was draining. Plagued by flashbacks to the point of saturation, I found it hard to separate the attacks and to work out what order they had occurred in. There were so many rapes, so many assaults, that they all merged into one long horror film. The officers said the word 'sex' so many times that the meaning became diluted and bleached. The word seemed to somehow lose its potency.

And as each memory resurfaced, my old life spun further and further away from me, like a child's toy, spinning faster and faster, until it was completely out of sight. I would never be able to go back to the girl I had once been. Even then, that was clear to me. And yet, alongside this new and heavy weariness, my child's view of the world prevailed.

'I've already admitted I was drinking alcohol,' I said. 'Will I get into trouble?'

I did not understand the insignificance of drinking alcohol. Or rather, I understood it only too well. Time and time again, in the interview, I blamed myself for what had happened to me, and it was the start of a pernicious pattern that would all but destroy me.

'I went along with it. I didn't want him to hurt me. It's all my fault because I'd been drinking.'

I told the officers that I made a phone call to a friend after that first assault in the churchyard.

'Who did you call?' they asked.

I squirmed with uncertainty, again, a childish view of adult horror.

'Do I have to mention it? Will you tell my mum?' I asked. 'I don't want her to know… Will he get into trouble?'

Eventually, with some encouragement, I told them about my 18-year-old friend, Paul, from Stockport, who I'd met online. I admitted meeting him in person too. They did not ask me more about him, and neither did I offer. My brain was so full of the previous night that I couldn't begin to think about him as well. In my mind, there was no connection at all between him and the attacks. Later, I would realise they were inextricably bound – one would not have existed without the other.

The questions continued and I shrunk smaller and smaller with each reply. I was disappearing right there, in the interview room. I felt like a flickering candle that could so easily be extinguished. More than anything, as the hours passed, I was desperate to have a wash. I was so uncomfortable in my own skin that I wanted to rip off the top layer and incinerate it.

Back at home, after the interview was finally over, I locked myself in the bathroom. Under the shower, I turned up the temperature until it was scalding and I scrubbed at my skin. My bruises were raw and swollen, especially on my neck and face. My mind flashed back uncomfortably to one of the attackers having sharp, uneven, teeth that dug into the sides of my mouth when he kissed me. I could feel an ulcer forming there already. Then I found the scratch from the man's ring. It stung under the hot water, but I scrubbed it regardless. I would never be clean again – I understood that. But I had to try. The fight had not gone from me yet, not quite.

Later, as I lay in bed, I had the oddest sensation that I was no longer the same girl, no longer the same shape or form. Dehumanised, I felt like the physical manifestation of white noise, just a collection of disruptive frequencies, without substance and without soul. Where had I gone? What had happened to me? Somehow, I fell into a troubled sleep, haunted by nightmares in which I was walking along a dark tree-lined path, with condoms hanging from the lower branches of the trees. Behind me, I heard the noise of a car, which, though I slowed my step, did not overtake me. Instead it followed slowly behind me, right on my heel.

'Don't look round, Sam,' I told myself. 'It's them. They're here. They're after you.'

My heart thumped as I broke into a run. No matter how many turns I took, and how slowly or quickly I ran, the car was always there, just behind me. I did not dare to look at it; I knew better than to turn around and face the occupants. But I could hear the car engine. I could sense them salivating as they weighed up their prize. I ran and ran, but the path went on and on and there were thousands of trees decorated with condoms. There was no end to it. When I woke, in a cold sweat, I had a moment of relief that my nightmare was over.

And then I realised it was only just beginning.

That afternoon, I was sitting in the living room in a trance, hardly able to knit together the past few days: the violence of the rapes, the violation of the police procedures, the monotony of a day on the sofa. Disparate events, with me at the centre. As I stared blankly into space, wondering how on earth I had landed myself in this catastrophic mess, the landline rang. The telephone was next to me, and reflexively, I answered.

'Hello?' asked a voice. 'Is that you – the girl from Friday night?'

My heart stuttered, and for a second, it seemed to forget how to beat. It was him. It was the driver. Without any doubt. Only at that moment I remembered I had given him my phone number. Only then, I realised he could easily work out where I lived. He had driven me to the edge of the estate, and he had my landline number. I was easily traceable, and I was not safe here. Wordlessly, I took the handset to my mother and gave it to her.

'Hello?' she said.

I was trembling so violently I could barely sit back down. The fear was so real I could taste it, metallic and cold. I felt like he was here, in my living room. I caught the sour whiff of his sweat in the air. I heard him laughing. I saw his eyes glittering like two black coals. He could find me. He could rape me again. Terrified, I ran upstairs to my bedroom, slamming the door shut and covering my head with my duvet.

'Leave me alone,' I sobbed. 'You had what you wanted. I can't take any more. Please leave me alone.'

The police came and took details of the call. But nothing they said could make me feel safe.

'Why isn't he in prison?' I asked. 'Why is he allowed to phone me?'

A few days later, I had to return to the police station for another interview. By now, I felt punch-drunk, numb with the repetition of the same things, over and over. The words sounded senseless, yet at the same time momentous.

They signalled the end of life as I knew it.

11

WHEN THE police interviews were over, I never wanted to leave the house again. I was terrified of seeing my attackers and, over time, this fear intensified to include seeing everyone I knew and anyone else besides. I became frightened of fresh air itself. Even a trip to the corner shop was an over-facing. I did not go out into the back garden, nor did I open my bedroom windows. It all felt like too much of a risk. My skin crawled as I imagined my attackers staking out the house in the dead of night, scaling the walls and climbing in through my open window as I slept. Sometimes I'd wake, sweating and sobbing, convinced there was someone standing over my bed.

Take off your clothes! Lie back and put your legs around my neck.

'Go away!' I screamed, even though there was nothing there except shadows. 'Go away!'

I was petrified in my own bedroom, yet conversely, I refused to leave it. Soon after the attacks, I had a scheduled hospital appointment to be tested for autism and Asperger's. I had been on the waiting list for so long and my parents were eager for me to attend. I wanted to stay at home. I had no interest in a diagnosis, or its impact on a future I no longer felt I had. But my parents insisted, and so, jittery and panicky, I found myself in a hospital waiting room. Scanning the face of everyone who walked past, I convinced myself, more than once, that I had spotted one of the men.

'There,' I gasped. 'The man with his back to us. I'm sure it's the passenger from the taxi.'

He turned around and, sagging with relief, I realised it wasn't him at all. But the respite was temporary.

'What about him?' I stammered, pointing out a man at the other end of the corridor. 'He looks like one of the men who waited outside the police station.'

But as he got nearer to us, I saw he wore doctors' scrubs and had a stethoscope around his neck. He looked nothing like my attacker. My mind was playing tricks on me. By the time I was called in for my appointment, I was a quivering wreck. The diagnostic testing for autism and Asperger's passed me by; my thoughts were elsewhere. But somehow, I managed to nod or shake my head in all the right places. Eventually, the consultant said to me:

'The test results show you have ADHD and Asperger's Syndrome.'

Numbly, I nodded.

'Do you have any questions?' she asked.

Numbly again, I shook my head.

I buttoned my coat and stood up. I just wanted to be back under my duvet and to be left alone. As a small girl, I'd been told I was too noisy for the world. Now the world was too noisy for me. But that afternoon, the social worker came and asked me to try going back to school.

'I can't,' I said flatly. 'I just can't.'

'Try to do just one morning,' she suggested. 'See how you feel. We can speak to the teachers and ensure they make allowances for you.'

I felt too weak to argue and, somehow, a couple of days later, I found myself walking through the entrance doors to school. I was very self-conscious about the bites on my neck, which had swelled into purple bruises, and so the teachers had agreed I could wear a scarf to cover them. But there was a chunk of my chin missing, too, where I had been bitten, and I couldn't cover that. Everywhere I went, I felt all eyes were on me, as the other kids whispered and gossiped behind my back. I wasn't sure how much they knew, if anything, of the attacks. No doubt the story had been passed around so much it now held very little of the truth. But even a small slice of truth was too much for me to share. I wanted to crawl under a desk and hide away from them all. Instead, I was under a spotlight, right at the centre of attention. Even the teachers seemed to give me a second, curious glance. At morning break, as I was walking down a corridor, I heard a teacher shout:

'Samantha Roberts! Remove your scarf. That's not part of school uniform and well you know it.'

I felt myself shrivel with shame.

'I have special permission, Sir,' I mumbled. 'I have a letter from the head.'

'We'll see about that,' he said grimly. 'Take it off now or you'll find yourself in detention.'

There was no way I could remove my scarf. The bites and

bruises would only add further fuel to the fire for the gossips. Besides, I'd been promised I could wear it.

'Samantha!' he said firmly, holding out his hand for my scarf. 'You either hand it over or you're in trouble. Last warning.'

'Yeah, whatever,' I muttered, already turning and heading for the doors. I walked straight out and straight home.

'I'm not going back,' I said to my parents. 'I can't do it.'

Climbing into bed, I wished fervently that I could unravel the past year. From a ball of knotted cotton, I longed to unwind every action that had led me to this wretched state. I wished I had never joined the teen website and never heard of Paul Waites. I wished I'd never gone to the churchyard, never got drunk, never gone to the police station. For a 12-year-old, I had a long list of regrets. And I blamed myself for them. I had bought the alcohol. I had made the MSN account. I had got in the car. I had to take the responsibility.

'Everyone thinks you're a slag, Sam,' I told myself fiercely. 'And that's because you are.'

My bruises healed as the days went by, but the mental wounds bled openly. Self-hatred and guilt sludged through me as I continued to hold myself to account. And nobody *at all ever* tried to correct that belief. If anything, it was rein-forced.

My physical health deteriorated, too, and I developed an ear infection, which the GP insisted was a tropical bug, and he said I could only have picked it up overseas. He was stumped when I announced I had never been abroad in my life. I felt sure the infection was somehow connected to the rapes, but I didn't know how. After several courses of anti-biotics, my ear only got worse. I was referred to the Royal Manchester Children's Hospital to have it treated weekly. I had to wear an ear patch too – another marker, another red flag, betraying that I was not the same as the other children. The scarf. The ear patch. The missing chunk of chin. They were merely outward signs of the sickness inside me.

I was also preoccupied by discomfort and irritation down below. And by the time I plucked up courage to confide in my mother, it was becoming unbearable. I couldn't go to the toilet without wincing in pain. Back at the GP surgery, it was feared I might have a sexually transmitted disease. Piled on top of all the other humiliations I had suffered, this was simply another twist of the knife. My dignity had long ago been smashed to pieces. The tests, thankfully, came back negative, and I was treated instead for a urine infection.

'Now that your neck and chin are looking better, you should try returning to school,' said my social worker.

But my physical injuries were simply the tip of it. My anxiety bubbled at the mere thought of going near the place again. My school was in the town centre, close to the churchyard where I had been assaulted and near to the Sainsbury's car park where I had been raped and the bus station where I had vomited afterwards. The area was a cesspit of memories, a geographical tapestry of suffering, stitched together by pain. I could not bear to physically make the journey to school, never mind sit through lesson after mind-numbing lesson.

'But what about your education?' my social worker asked.

'What about it?' I replied flatly. 'That's the least of my worries.'

A psychiatric report soon after withdrew the diagnosis of Asperger's and replaced it instead with one of autism. It made no difference to me. There was little support offered and there were no pathways for me to follow. The report stated that I was 'particularly vulnerable to being led into inappropriate behaviours'.

As an adult, the irony hits me hard. If I was especially susceptible, why had nobody protected me? Why had the attacks been allowed to happen in the first place? How did I slip through so many holes in so many nets into so much danger? But aged 12, I dismissed the diagnosis, pulled the duvet over my head and wished I could magic myself away. The world was too unfriendly and too unkind. I remembered the airing cupboard in my old bedroom as a small girl, the warmth, the wheaty smell of the home brew. I pictured again Granny Pat's comfy sofa, balancing my bowl of cereal as I watched our favourite whodunnit on the TV. I wished, how I wished, I was back there now.

One morning, my mother stayed off work and a police officer came to see us. He explained that tests on my clothes, my body, the condoms from the house and the bedding had shown several semen samples. But they had been able to match only two. One was the driver of the taxi, a man called Shakil Chowdhury. He was 39 years old, much older than he had claimed. But amongst his many atrocities, that hardly seemed to matter. The rapist from the first house had been arrested too, but had been granted bail and, an illegal immigrant, he had subsequently disappeared. The police were unable to find him.

'What about all the others?' I asked. 'The men from outside the police station? The man from the churchyard? All the men at the second house?'

'I am really sorry,' the officer said.

'So the others all go unpunished?' I asked incredulously. 'Every single one? They just get away with everything?'

Only in that moment did it hit me just how vital it was for each attacker to be brought to justice. It had not even occurred to me that the police would not be able to find and charge them. I had been through those excruciating interviews, the pain and humiliation of the physical examinations, the journey around Oldham to relive the attacks. I had picked out houses and a car. And for what? Only Chowdhury was in custody. The man from the first house had most likely fled overseas. The other men had simply melted away, free to reoffend.

On that night, I had been driven around Oldham town centre, late at night when the roads were quiet, in two separate vehicles. I had been ensnared by two men right outside the police station and one of the men had himself been inside the police station. Yet it appeared there was not a single piece of CCTV evidence to be found. There were no witnesses. There was nothing. I had identified routes, a car, houses. I had given physical descriptions of my attackers. And yet, despite searches which included seizing condoms, towels and bedsheets, they had been unable to match the DNA with anyone other than Chowdhury and the suspect who had later fled. Added to this, the police had access to

Chowdhury's personal effects, including his phone, with his lists of contacts, calls and messages. It beggared belief that they had found absolutely nothing.

'They just get away with it?' I repeated numbly, as if by saying it again, the answer might somehow change.

'We will continue to do all we can,' the officer said, as he stood up to leave.

If I had felt desolate before, then now, I sank even further. I felt worthless. Utterly pointless. Even the police didn't take me seriously. Even they didn't care about what I had been through. This felt like yet another violation, another kick in the face. I didn't matter to the men, and I didn't matter to the police. I didn't matter *at all*. And the lack of arrests and charges only reinforced my belief that I was to blame. The police didn't seem to think it was worth tracking down the attackers, so they must think I was to blame too.

'They think you're a slut,' I told myself. *'You're just a stupid kid.'*

And if my attackers remained free to roam the streets, how would I ever be safe? Chowdhury had my phone number. He could work out where I lived. He had probably already done so. He could send the other men to attack me, to silence me – even to murder me.

Nausea roared up my throat and I swallowed hard. No, I would never be safe again. And how would any other child be safe? They could target another young girl, it could be someone I knew, and it could be happening right now. The thought made me physically sick. With my rapists on the loose, free to prowl, I became fixated on the attacks. I could think of nothing else.

My memories flicked back over the way each section of that night had fallen neatly into place, almost as though it was co-ordinated. I remembered the way the bedrooms seemed pre-prepared, as if they had been planning for my arrival – the towels spread across the pillows, the packet of condoms in the child's bedroom, the duvet moved from the bed. I was not their first victim, I was certain of that. And I would not be the last. These men were serial predators, part of a dark and dangerous paedophile ring. And now, with the exception of Shakil Chowdhury, they were free to continue exactly as before. I had thought that speaking to the police was the right thing to do, but it felt like I had completely wasted my time.

For many months – years even – I marvelled grimly at what I saw as the many coincidences that led from one attack to the next, as though they were completely separate and unrelated. Only in later years, I realised they were inextricably and causally linked. Right from being eight years old, the rape by The Man made me susceptible to the attack by The Boy. With my self-esteem eroding, I had grasped with gratitude the attention Paul Waites had showed me. After he raped me, my self-worth had been shattered.

Then, on that fateful night, I'd got into one car after another, passed from one predator to the next. It had, retrospectively, felt like the set of a horror film, with the two men conveniently hanging around outside the police station, the next man appearing as if by magic from a house, the next two men popping up along the main road where I was walking. Every moment was staged; it was all planned. They knew I was alone and vulnerable, and like vultures they had swooped. I had flashed up on their radar like an easy bargain, a drunk teenager, naive and scared. This was why the bedroom was prepared and ready, why the condoms were in the drawer, why the towels were across the pillows, why the duvet had been removed from the bed.

There was no coincidence. None at all.

12

DESPITE ENCOURAGEMENT from my teachers and social services, I could not bear to return to school again. The journey itself was fraught with reminders and landmarks that flashed me right back to the trauma of the attacks. On a couple of occasions, my parents drove me to school as I lay down flat on the back seat to avoid looking out. But once I arrived at the school gates, my panic skyrocketed several levels as each memory resurfaced. The library. The Sainsbury's car park. The churchyard.

The school building itself loomed over me like a giant bully, bearing down on me even before I stepped inside. I did not feel safe outside those walls, but neither did I feel safe inside. I couldn't breathe in my lessons, let alone learn anything.

'I'm not going back,' I said.

But even at home, I no longer felt secure. My bedroom had once been a safe haven, and I had enjoyed the distractions of devising different colour schemes and design ideas. I adored my day bed, and my fluffy rug, and my cats snoozing on my windowsill. But now, I was constantly checking the windows and doors, unable to relax. Every time I heard a noise outside, I froze, fearing the men were back to get me. The driver, Chowdhury, had been charged and was on remand. But the other men were all free. What if Chowdhury wanted revenge for me speaking to the police and he sent the others to my home? They could murder me, my parents and my cats. What if they murdered Granny Pat too? Aged 12, everything seemed possible. Nothing seemed out of the question. I was in fear for my life.

I was worrying about my future, while at the same time I was trapped in the past. Flashbacks from the attacks snapped at my heels like the jaws of rabid dogs. During fretful nights' sleep, I found myself back in the Nissan with Shakil Chowdhury and his passenger.

'No way you're 12! Of course we'll take you home… get into the back seat'

I relived each segment of the journey, blaming myself that I did not jump out at a junction, or scream for help from the car window. Or, more simply, I reproached myself for ever getting into the taxi at all.

It's your fault, Sam. You got it. You deserved what you got. You always make a mess of everything.

In my nightmares, I watched the Bumbly Bee lampshade swinging back and forth, back and forth, back and forth. I pictured in vivid technicolour that green and yellow bedroom with its matching curtains and duvet set. And with a stab of concern, I remembered the condoms in the drawer. I worried so much about the child who slept in that bedroom. I hoped, more than anything, they were safe. I hoped social services had protected them in a way they had not protected me. And even in my dreams, I burned with shame as I was made to strip naked and lie flat under the lampshade. I choked back tears as the attackers bit at my face and neck like I was a slab of steak. And I cringed in humiliation when that man made his nasty jibe about my weight.

'You have a big belly'

Often when I awoke, I could feel the weight of them still, flattening my lungs and crushing the life from me. I could smell them too, the miasma of dried-in sweat, sour breath and stale cigarette smoke. Turning my face into the pillow, I wept and wept and longed to be back in my childhood home with my kittens and my Groovy Chick walls and my airing cupboard. I needed somewhere to hide, and yet, as I would later learn, I could not hide from myself. Locked in a spinning maelstrom of stultifying fear and shame, I saw no way forward and no way out.

One morning after a shower, I picked up a razor blade from the side of the sink and ran it lightly down my arm. It was enough just to snag the skin in a few places and, as bubbles of blood oozed from my wounds, I was overwhelmed with feelings of relief. As I bled out, I also breathed out, filling my starved lungs with oxygen. The pain was, paradoxically, a comfort to me. My shoulders relaxed and my eyes closed, as the tension in my bones slackened and eased. The cool feeling of the blood on the surface of my skin was a true solace. I told myself I would not do it again. This was just a one-off, a special exception on a bad day. But a couple of days later, I was back in the bathroom.

'Just a scratch,' I told myself. 'One scratch and then that's enough.'

But the next morning, I woke to another bad day, and I self-harmed again. It became addictive, and as the pressure built within me, the cuts in my arms became a release, replacing, or at least obscuring, the mental agony in my head with physical pain. As the blood flowed, I somehow felt I was drawing down on my anguish and setting it free.

I began harming myself most days, telling myself a small nick was all I needed to get through the next few hours. But as time went on, my tolerance grew, and I needed more. One day, I scratched my arm until there was a steady stream of blood dripping from my vein and splashing on to the floor tiles. In a trance, I stood and watched as crimson blood trickled into the grouting and formed rivulets. Only when I heard a key in the door did I snap to my senses, wrapping my arm in a towel and pulling my dressing gown over the top, before hastily cleaning the floor. I did not want anyone to know, least of all my parents.

'You ok?' my mother called from the hallway.

'Yes, fine,' I replied breezily.

My social worker had told me I was attention-seeking. Little did she know the lengths I went to in order to deflect the attention elsewhere. One morning, I woke up feeling even worse than usual. The bare facts alone were horrific. The rapes. The sexual assaults. The grooming. But it was the smaller details that floored me: the Bumbly Bee lampshade, Chowdhury telling me to clean myself, the man laughing at my belly. The scenes played on a loop inside my head, over and over, faster and faster, until I could take no more. It was like being stuck on a white-knuckle ride and not being allowed to get off. My mouth watered as I retched and ran to the bathroom. Hanging over the toilet, with the sour taste of bile on my tongue, I felt I'd had enough. Blindly, reflexively, I opened the cleaning cupboard and wrenched the safety top off a bottle of bleach.

'What are you doing?' my dad yelled, running in from the landing as I tipped the bottle into my mouth.

He snatched it from me, and I felt the bleach burn my tongue and throat as he dragged me to the sink, splashing water in my face and mouth.

'You'll be okay. Don't worry. You'll be okay,' he said.

But I did not want to be okay. I did not even want to *be*. In hospital, I was made to drink copious amounts of fluid. I had scans and blood tests, which came back clear, before being referred for a psychiatric assessment. I was allowed home that same night.

'Promise you won't do this again,' my parents said, and I nodded my head and promised.

But just a few weeks later, again lost in a fog of intolerable pain, I swallowed a full packet of painkillers. I was rushed back to hospital, and when I woke, my mouth was dry, and my stomach felt like it had been scraped out and emptied of every last ounce of nourishment.

'What's happened?' I asked groggily.

'You've had your stomach pumped,' a nurse told me as she plumped my pillows. 'You could have died. You're a young girl with your life ahead of you. Please don't do this again. Things will get better, I promise you.'

She had a kind, careworn face and I knew she meant well.

But I did not feel young. I did not feel my life was ahead of me. And I definitely did not believe things would get better. I felt somehow out of reach, stranded down a long and twisty tunnel, as though it was too late for me. As though my chance at life had come and gone and I had missed it. Again, I was sent home with the promise of psychological support. But I was sick of adults promising me things they didn't deliver. The way I saw it, the social workers, the police, my family, had all let me down.

Another day, consumed with self-loathing and guilt, I punched a section of wall in my bedroom, which was decorated with textured plaster. The ridges ripped my knuckles, and they bled all over my T-shirt. Grabbing a tea towel, I ran from the house to Grandad Frank's across the street.

'What's all this?' he asked gently, dabbing my injuries with cotton wool and warm water and fixing me up with a bandage around each hand.

'I fell over,' I told him, staring at my shoes.

'Well, anytime you fall over, you can come to me,' he replied. 'I'll always be here for you, Samantha.'

There was such sadness in his voice that it pulled at my heartstrings. I had seen very little of Grandad Frank or of Granny Pat since the attacks. I hadn't seen anyone, really. As much as I was hiding myself away, I also suspected I was being hidden away. Were they trying to keep me safe or was everyone ashamed of me? Did they blame me as I blamed myself? My weekend visits to Granny Pat had dried up, partly because I didn't want to leave the house, but partly also because nobody had arranged for me to go. Nobody ever suggested I could visit her.

As these monsters had taken over my life, everyone I held dear had left it. And again, I felt as though nobody cared.

13

SHAKIL CHOWDHURY was due to stand trial in the summer of the following year. Because he was pleading not guilty, I was warned I would have to give evidence, via video link. A few weeks before the case was due to start, an officer took me to Minshull Street Crown Court in Manchester to look around. I had never been inside a court building in my life. And though I wanted Chowdhury to pay for what he had done, I was also wary of speaking out against him, especially knowing that his associates were still free. The officer reassured me I'd be giving evidence on a screen, in a different area of the building, and so I wouldn't have to be in the same room as him. I wouldn't have to see or hear him at all. But just the thought of him being nearby, of him hearing my voice and knowing I was helping to send him to jail, was terrifying.

After my visit to the court building, I had recurring nightmares in which I gave my evidence, as arranged, through the video link. But the judge became annoyed because I didn't speak loudly enough and ordered a policeman to bring me into the courtroom in person. When I took my place in the witness box, I saw to my confusion that Chowdhury was in the judge's wig and robes, and underneath I spotted he was wearing my FCUK jacket.

'It's him!' I yelled. 'That's the rapist! He has the same cruel eyes, the bushy eyebrows. I know it's him! He's even wearing my jacket!'

Chowdhury leaned across towards me and prodded my arm with a long, yellow fingernail. Close up, I saw filth crusted underneath.

'You say one word against me, and I'll hang your cats from your washing line and slit their throats,' he hissed. 'Just one word.'

I woke with a pain in my arm, convinced I had a scratch where he had poked me with his fingernail.

'It was a dream,' I reminded myself. 'Stop being silly.'

Even so, I pulled on my dressing gown and crept downstairs to check on my four cats, sleeping in their bed in the kitchen. They were safe – for now.

On the morning of the trial, we were almost late leaving as I shepherded my cats inside. I knew it was a dream. But I also knew Chowdhury and his gang were monsters. Evil personified. They would stop at nothing to get what they wanted and I bore the scars of that. My mother and my aunt came with me to the court hearing. We were signed in and then shown into a basement room, which was already bustling with other families.

In one corner, there were children playing on an Xbox. In another, there was a box of toys and books. At first, I was overawed simply by how busy it was. I'd been holed up at home for so long, I wasn't used to this. Taking deep breaths,

I told myself it was just like a hospital waiting room. I could almost convince myself I was here for an autism assessment, or a check-up for my ear infection. But my stomach was cramping with stress. I was gripping my chair so hard that my fingertips were white. I imagined Chowdhury in this same building somewhere, waiting for his trial to begin. Closing my eyes, I saw with startling detail his bushy eyebrows and his cold, cruel eyes.

'You must wash yourself because I like cleanliness.'

He was probably seething with fury, raging that I had dared to make a complaint against him. I remembered my dream, the way his filthy fingernail, curled at the end, had raked down my arm as he threatened to kill my cats. The man was wicked. I didn't need a nightmare to tell me that. Had I done the right thing coming here? Was it worth the risk? And even now, even in a court of law, I felt I was somehow at fault. My fingertips were sore by the time a barrister called my mother into a different room. A few minutes later, I was called in too.

'Your attacker has pleaded guilty,' the barrister explained. 'It's good news because you won't have to give evidence. You can go home.'

The moment I heard the word 'guilty', I felt my knees buckle with sheer relief. It was over. It was over at last. He would be sent to prison for a very long time and perhaps I could start to put this horrible ordeal behind me. Arriving home, I ran around the house to cuddle each cat in turn – Megan, Piper, Sox and Spot.

'It's over,' I told them. 'He's going to prison forever.'

In preparation for the sentencing hearing, I wrote a statement.

The first few months after the rape, I felt lonely and didn't want to go out as I was frightened I would be attacked again and that I would see the person who raped me whilst I was out. I couldn't go to school for a long time as it was nearby where the start of it happened. I was also worried what people in school might say… Even now I don't want to leave the house. I still feel horrible, I am scared all the time and keep having flashbacks… the only way I will feel safe is if the man who raped me is sent to prison for life.

I did not, for a minute, imagine any other outcome than a life sentence. He had raped me multiple times and he had brought his friends to rape me too. A man like that did not deserve ever to be freed.

On August 31 2007, Chowdhury appeared again before Minshull Street Crown Court. Though I was at home, I waited nervously by the telephone for news. When the officer called, her voice was uncertain.

'He's been sent to jail for six years, Sam,' she told me. 'I'm sorry it's not longer.'

'Six years?' I asked. 'In total? Are you sure?'

He wouldn't serve his full sentence, the police had already explained that to me. So it didn't even work out at one year per rape. Even after all the disappointments and let-downs from the police investigation, I had once again trusted the system blindly. I had expected him to go to jail for the rest of his life. After all, the rest of my life was ruined because of him.

In shock, I ended the call, with my mind casting about

for a form of relief. I needed a bottle of cider. Or a razor to release my pain. Anything to escape the torment inside my own head. My mother, sensing my distress, suggested we could go out to pick up something she'd bought on eBay and maybe get a burger on the way back. Desperate for distraction, I agreed. The radio was on in the car and as the hourly news came on, I froze.

'A 39-year-old man has been jailed for just six years after raping a child. Shakil Chowdhur..'

My mother leaned across to snap the radio off, but it was too late. With my head down, I watched as the tears splashed from my face and on to my hands. I had left the house to escape this, but it was following me around. I was under siege. It felt to me like Chowdhury was the lucky one, safe in prison without these constant reminders. And they were not done yet.

Reports in the evening paper confirmed Chowdhury had pleaded guilty to six counts of rape and had been sentenced to six years for each, to be served concurrently. The report revealed I had been 'plied with drink and passed between four men' who took turns to rape me. It said Chowdhury had raped me a total of 11 times, using different beds at the house and forcing me to clean myself between attacks. He had also invited other men to rape me. In the report, Norman Brennan, director of the Victims of Crime Trust, said:

'This sentence is almost as disgusting as the crime itself. Gang rape is the most despicable and appalling crime. Judges surely have a duty of care to punish people guilty of such crimes and send out a serious

message to others who might contemplate such action. In my opinion this has done neither.'

After the sentencing, Detective Chief Inspector Mary Doyle from Oldham CID said:

'This child was subjected to a terrifying and prolonged attack from Chowdhury and his associates. One of the first things she told him was her age, so there is no doubt that he was aware how young she was. Chowdhury's actions that evening would have been unacceptable on a woman of any age, but to carry out this sort of attack on a 12-year-old child is simply abhorrent. His victim has shown a great deal of bravery throughout this case, informing the police and pursuing this case to prosecution. I hope her bravery and the resulting conviction will encourage other victims to come forward, safe in the knowledge that GMP [Greater Manchester Police] *will investigate any complaints fully and take robust action against the people responsible.'*

I wanted to rip the newspaper into pieces. This was a farce, a kick in the teeth. How could the police claim to investigate all complaints fully when eight of my attackers were still out there, walking the streets? And how could the court case be viewed as 'robust action' when Chowdhury had been sentenced to just six years in prison for repeatedly raping a child, and arranging for others to rape me too?

It was not enough to say I was disappointed or disillusioned. I felt violated, victimised and trodden on. I had been a fool to trust the authorities and the justice system. But I would make sure that did not happen again.

The anniversary of the attack came around in October 2007, and my parents suggested we could go out for a meal. Dully, I agreed. But when the day came, I could not leave my room. I felt as though I was pinned to the bed, paralysed with shock, whilst re-runs of that horrific night played across an imaginary projector overhead.

'Fancy a snog?'

'Do you want to get in our car and chill for a bit.'

'Take your clothes off.'

'How are you getting home? Here is 84p. Here is what you're worth.'

'You have a big belly.'

'You must wash yourself because I like cleanliness.'

Would I ever be free of these men? Would I ever be free of myself?

14

THE NEW school year had started and still, I could not face returning.

My friends' lives were all moving on as teenagers' should. They sat exams, they met up for burgers and milkshakes, they bought make-up, they got boyfriends. These were ghostly, ephemeral reminders of a life I could have had, of a normality that had once awaited me, but had evaporated after the rapes. I'd always thought I might like to be a police officer when I grew up. I'd hoped to study textiles for GCSE – I might have ended up working in design. But those plans would never take shape now. That old path had fallen away, eroded by pain, and I would never know who I might have become or what I could have achieved. My own existence remained suspended. I had been on pause since the attacks, caught in amber, like a helpless, fragile insect. Like the poor little Bumbly Bee on the lampshade.

'Samantha, you need to return to school,' my social worker said. 'It's been a year.'

'I just can't,' I said. 'I'm not ready.'

If anything, as time passed, I felt worse than before. My GP suggested counselling might help and I agreed. I didn't want to be stuck, like a stopped clock, and if there was a way forward, I was willing to try it. After a referral was made, a counsellor named Hayley came to our home.

'What do you like doing, Sam?' she asked me.

But the question just confused me. I felt anesthetised; stupefied. I could not think of anything I liked to do at all. It took two weeks before I could think of an answer.

'Films,' I told her. 'I like watching films.'

My parents already had a subscription for LoveFilm so I could rent DVDs without having to leave the house. I bought a few of my favourite ones, and I soon amassed quite a collection. Every day, after breakfast, I returned to my room to start watching a film. At first, it was almost impossible to concentrate. My mind felt calcified and impenetrable, as if I was under sedation. But as time passed, I became engrossed in plot lines and characters, despite myself. The rest of the world, along with all my problems, melted away as my films offered a portal into another life. A better life.

I loved all the old Disney favourites, and the little girl in me still delighted in the tale of the princess finding her prince. It would never happen for me. I had accepted that. But the next best thing was to share in someone else's happiness. I enjoyed rom-coms, too, classic girl-meets-boy stories. At heart, I was still a romantic, even though my head told me otherwise.

I got into watching boxsets such as *Torchwood, Merlin* and *Buffy the Vampire Slayer.* I had a lot of time on my hands, so I was willing to watch most things. I had only two rules: no horror and no documentaries. I was trying to forget my own horror, not indulge in more. And I didn't want to watch any true life, because that was exactly what I was trying to escape.

As the weeks passed, my collection grew and grew, and I spent hours painstakingly arranging my films by genre, and then alphabetically, on the bookcase in my room. Each film was neatly categorised and ordered. I loved the organisational aspect almost as much as watching the films, because it gave me a form of control in a world where I had none. It offered order amongst the chaos.

'You're doing well,' said my social worker. 'You're making progress.'

And she was right. I thought less about ending my life and more about the upcoming season of *Buffy*. But at the same time, I was living in a fantasy world, existing vicariously through the characters I saw on the screen.

By now, I was 14 years old – a teenager. It was a time when typically I should have been branching out socially and emotionally, putting out feelers beyond the boundaries of my family. Instead, I was spending that time in complete isolation. I did not see my friends or anyone at all my own age. In one way, I was like a small child again, unable to leave the house unaccompanied, spending hours in my bedroom and surrounded by the comfort of my own familiar things. My days were reassuringly samey and predictable, like a re-run of one of my favourite boxsets. Yet I also felt much older than my peers. I had no interest in going out, in boyfriends or in new clothes. I felt disenchanted, weary and jaded. I had bypassed my teenage years completely and landed somewhere on the other side. Somewhere very lonely indeed.

Alongside my lack of socialising, I was getting no education, and neither did I want any. I did not look any further than my next film. For me, that was taxing enough. But the adults around me were becoming increasingly concerned and it was decided I should be taught at home. The tutor who came soon afterwards was a lovely lady who did her best to help salvage what was left of my school days.

'I thought you might like to visit a museum,' she suggested.

I stared at her in alarm.

'Leave the house?' I asked.

She nodded gently.

'I will be with you,' she said.

At the root of my fear of going outside was the terror of being spotted by one of my attackers. It never occurred to me that they, the aggressors, should be frightened of bumping into me. The usual misgivings ran around my head. The men had my phone number – they could easily find out where I lived and ambush me as I left the house. And who would I turn to if I were attacked again? Not the social services. Not the police. Not the courts. I had learnt my lesson there. I had never before worn make-up but, on the day of our museum trip, I rifled through my mother's make-up bag and applied layer after layer of foundation, eyeshadow, blusher and mascara. My aim was not especially to look good. My aim was to not look like myself. I hoped, with enough make-up, I might be completely unrecognisable. And as I stared at myself in the bathroom mirror, I was pleased to see a stranger looking back.

'Wow!' my tutor smiled. 'You look amazing, Sam.'

Despite my nerves, the museum trip went well. History had been one of my favourite subjects at school and I enjoyed learning about the Industrial Revolution and the way Northern towns had grown. And I felt somehow protected underneath all my make-up, as though I were in disguise. It was a little like being in fancy dress. I was careful not to talk loudly, or to be overheard, so that my voice could not be recognised.

Arriving home, I had to admit I'd enjoyed my day out, and I was looking forward to another. That weekend, I persuaded my mother to take me to Superdrug, to pick out my own colours and brands of make-up. We had a look around Boots, too. I became totally engrossed. This was like decorating my bedroom, only this time, I was decorating my face. I picked out some wash-in, wash-out hair dyes along with my new make-up.

'I'm going pink next week,' I decided. 'Nobody will know who I am.'

I lost myself in eyeshadow palettes and make-up brushes and it was sweet therapy just to have a couple of hours away from my constant worrying. On our trip home, I switched back on to high alert, scanning the streets for any man who looked like any one of my attackers. Time after time, I thought I spotted someone. But I was always mistaken. And over time, their faces blurred and merged so that I could not be sure who was who. I didn't want to hang on to my memories, yet it felt like a damning indictment that I could not remember the faces of my rapists. Again, I saw this as my fault. Again, I blamed myself.

'How are you ever going to catch them if you don't remember them?' I asked myself.

But the truth was that they would never be caught, because nobody was looking for them. All I could do, in the meantime, was make sure they didn't come looking for me and so my morning make-up routine quickly became the most important part of my day. Whether or not I was planning to leave my bedroom was immaterial, I needed my make-up as a shield. Each day, I hid behind a mask, layering blusher and eyeshadow on to my layers of pain, but not wanting to admit that I was, above all else, hiding from myself. On another trip to the make-up counters, I came across an offer for a free makeover if I spent £25.

'Go on then,' Mum smiled.

I loved having my make-up professionally done, and that gave me ideas of how to do it myself in the future. I bought new eyeliners and lip glosses, and I practised for hours in the bathroom mirror. But no matter how polished and perfect my face was, I never felt attractive. I never felt proud of the reflection that stared back at me from the mirror. All I ever saw was a girl on the run. A girl who needed to look like someone else. I dyed my hair on a weekly basis, a range of outrageous colours, from dark to blonde to bright pink and back again. Hardly a week passed by when I wasn't trying out a new shade. It was, I convinced myself, like having a whole new identity. My attackers would never find me now. And some days, I really felt I didn't know this new girl in the bathroom mirror with her pink hair and bright eyeshadow. Could I ever leave the old me behind and, more importantly, all that she had been through? Could I bury my trauma under so many layers of make-up that it would never resurface?

One day, my tutor suggested a trip to an art exhibition, and, with my hair dyed and face painted, I was filled with a false confidence, which I was getting better at faking.

'I'm looking forward to it,' I smiled.

But as we drove towards the town centre, my skin suddenly began to itch with unease.

'Where are we going?' I asked. 'Where's the exhibition?'

'It's in the town library,' she smiled. 'Just by Sainsbury's. In fact, we can park there if we buy something from the shop.'

Suddenly, I felt as though the passenger seat had collapsed from under me, and I was in free-fall.

'No,' I stuttered. 'No, I'm sorry. I can't go in. Not the library and not Sainsbury's. Take me home, please. Don't take me into the town centre. I really can't go to the exhibition. I'm sorry.'

But it was too late. We turned a corner and there it was. In a flash, I saw myself standing on the walkway with my drumsticks in my hand. I visualised Paul Waites sauntering towards me in his bandana without a care in the world. I watched myself retching against the pillar at the bus station after he had forced himself on me in the rape.

'Take me home,' I sobbed. 'Please take me home now.'

15

AFTER THE library trip, my educational days out went the same way as my education. My behaviour was challenging and distressing and I felt deeply sorry for my tutor. She had done her best for me. I was a difficult child, I knew. I had been told that often enough.

The home tutoring ended, but I continued to see my counsellor, Hayley, every three weeks. She came up with a suggestion of driving me along the school run and then stopping at the point I requested and turning back around. At first, I was set against it. It sounded like a trap to me.

'Nobody is going to force you to go to school,' she insisted. 'You don't even need to wear your uniform. We're just going to drive the route, as far as you feel comfortable, and then we'll come home.'

I liked Hayley and felt she was the only person I could trust.

'Okay,' I agreed.

But even leaving the house was fraught. I had become a virtual hermit except for my infrequent trips to buy make-up or to attend a doctor's appointment. The mere thought of stepping outside the front door and getting into Hayley's car was enough to send my heart rate racing.

'The fresh air will do you good,' my mother remarked, as I buttoned my coat.

I nodded. But as the cold air hit my face, my chest tightened, and I found I was struggling to breathe. I needed the reassurance of walls around me, of a duvet over my head, of a familiar film playing in the background.

'I can't do it,' I muttered.

'You can,' Hayley said, holding out her hand. 'Yes, you can.'

That first journey, we made it only as far as the second junction. And then, my resolve dissolved into a puddle around me.

'I need to go home,' I gasped, gripping the side of the seat. 'Please.'

True to her word, Hayley turned the car around and drove me straight back.

'We'll try again another day,' she said. 'You did well, Sam.'

It became part of my routine, driving towards – and never reaching – the school gates. One morning, I spotted the churchyard through the trees, and I had a panic attack, my ears buzzing loudly and my heart clattering against my ribcage. And there I was, catapulted right back to that day – the man with the umbrella asking me for a light, the predators outside the police station, the officer in the hi-vis jacket.

'Go home, sober up, and come back with an adult.'

How different it could have been if my complaint had been recorded there and then and I had not been sent out of the police station to walk straight into the lair of the two waiting paedophiles. But I could not dwell on that now. I had to move forwards.

'You're making progress,' Hayley assured me. 'It just takes time.'

Another day, we were stopped in traffic, and as we inched slowly forwards, I caught a distant view of the library through the houses. I was so frightened I snapped my seatbelt open and got out of the car.

'I can't,' I said breathlessly. 'I can't do it.'

Hayley turned the car around, coaxed me back in, and drove me home.

'Don't worry,' she said. 'You're safe now.'

In one respect, the trips were doing me good. I was becoming desensitised to the first part of the journey, which was the roads leading to the town centre. But as soon as we drew near to the school, the library, the churchyard and the Sainsbury's supermarket, I lost all control. And no matter how hard I tried and how much I wanted to beat my demons, they flared up every time, and every time, they defeated me. I did not know how to smash that final hurdle. I had been out of mainstream schooling for 18 months when I was given a place at a special education unit in Oldham. It was a distance away from the town centre, and therefore far away from all of the reminders and triggers of the past.

'Samantha, you have to give this a try,' my social worker said.

I knew everyone was working hard to try to help. My mother gave up her job so she could drive me to and from school. Everyone was full of encouragement and positivity. I was determined to give it my best shot.

The centre itself was not like a school, but there was none-theless a routine and a set of rules. At first, I was resentful. I'd spent over a year in my bedroom doing exactly what I wanted. I was in a routine of watching films all day and I wasn't used to teachers telling me what to do any more. But in other ways, it was nothing at all like I was expecting. I was free to leave a lesson when I felt pressured. I was allowed to smoke on the premises. I wasn't expected to wear a uniform. There was little focus on exams and academic achievement and, contrarily, I found myself wanting to sit maths and English GCSE. Even though my education was in tatters, there was still a small sliver of hope inside me – a voice, no matter how faint, urging me not to give up completely. Luckily, I had a strict English teacher who supported me and loaded me up with homework.

'Have these done by Monday,' she said, handing me a list of essay questions. 'And no excuses.'

Through her, I started to read. I loved Greek myths and supernatural stories. They were, like my films, a form of escape. I became entranced by the stories of Jason and the Argonauts, and Perseus and Andromeda. My favourite myth was of Icarus, who flew too close to the sun and died. Though it was sad, I loved the romance of his escape plan, and I wished I had one too. In my head, I went on adventures, I flew through the sky, I sailed across oceans, and I fought the creatures of the underworld. My books were a chance to forget, just for an hour or so, that I was me.

I made friends at the new school too, though we never met up outside lessons. Apart from my time at the unit, I was practically housebound. Each afternoon, I arrived home, double-locked the doors and sank to the floor with relief that another day was almost done. To the outside world, I was making baby steps of progress. But inwardly, my attackers were still intent on ruining me, unpicking me thread by thread, until there were gaping holes inside me. I felt I would never be whole again.

After months of me pestering my parents, we moved to a new home shortly before I turned 15. Paradoxically, though I had cherished the safety and solitude of my old bedroom, I was glad to leave it behind. The memories were ingrained into every piece of furniture, and each room held a toxic secret. I'd first spoken to Paul Waites on the teenage website in the small pantry off the hallway. In the living room, I'd taken the call from Shakil Chowdhury, the day after the rapes. In the bathroom, I'd cut my arms with the razor, and I'd drunk bleach. And in my bedroom, I'd harboured dark and desperate thoughts that had almost beaten me. The house itself looked downcast to me. The blank windows were like sad eyes. It was as though the walls understood the weight of misery they carried within.

In our new home, a few miles away, I had a larger bedroom with a small walk-in closet. I picked out black floral wallpaper and floor-length black curtains, which Megan loved to wrap herself up in. She was getting old and spent most of her days lazing under the curtains. I had a three-quarter-size bed, with a desk and chair, and a set of drawers. I had hoped, in our new house, in a new area, that I would finally be away from danger. Away from the old estate where Chowdhury knew my phone number. I had kidded myself that I could start again. That I could simply cover up the pain and the worry of the past with a fresh coat of paint and a new carpet. But that first night, as I got into bed, I felt a shiver of unease. Pushing aside the curtains, I peered out into the dark street.

'Do they know I'm here?' I asked Megan softly. 'Am I really safe? Am I?'

The sad truth was, I didn't feel it. I didn't feel safe in my own skin. I was just as cautious and alert as before, still always checking the street before I left the house and convincing myself that every man I saw was a potential predator. The stress was draining, and my energy and enthusiasm from the move were slowly leaching away. Meanwhile, the pressure inside me had built and built and I needed a new release.

At first, my walk-in wardrobe had seemed like a bonus grown-up addition to my new room. But I soon discovered it was also the perfect place to hide with a razor. I locked myself away in the dark, hacking at my arms and soaking up the blood from my injuries with an old towel.

I grew to hate my new bedroom, as it became synonymous with pain and harm and the foolishness of thinking I could run away from my past. Our new house had a spare bedroom, much smaller than mine, but I asked if I could move. My bed fit in there, just about, along with my desk and chair. I painted the walls baby blue, and we bought curtains of a darker blue. I began a project, cutting out images of the celebs I liked from my weekly magazines, *Heat* and *OK!*, and building up a collage on my bedroom wall. I used a glue gun to set them in place and, as the weeks went by, the collage grew and grew until it was sprawling across the entire wall. Like my books and my films, this was another escape. I wanted to be these celebrities and I wanted their lives.

Or rather, I didn't want to be me… with my life.

16

FOR MY 15th birthday, in December 2008, Granny Pat sent me a card and some money. I questioned again why she and I had lost contact and, instead of sending her a thank-you text message, I decided to go and see her. The moment she opened the door, her face creased into that familiar smile, and she held out her arms to me.

'I know you don't like cuddles, but I insist,' she beamed. 'I've missed you so much. I hope you've packed your pyjamas for a sleepover.'

She and I took up exactly where we had left off. We began a new tradition of card nights every Friday, playing rummy and blackjack to win a few pence. Though I was a little old for sleepovers, I enjoyed spending my evenings there. And most of all, I enjoyed our cereal suppers, balanced on our knees, as together we mulled over the likely culprit in the latest series of *Jonathan Creek*. Granny Pat never spoke of the attacks. That was not her way. But one night, as we settled down for an episode of *A Touch Of Frost*, she said to me:

'Please don't think I didn't care, Samantha. I always cared and I always thought of you.'

Her words were a salve for my bruised soul. Just to know

she cared, and that she loved me, meant the world to me. Thanks to Granny Pat, I became more confident at leaving the house on my own. I even started getting the bus to her place on Friday evenings. She helped me more than she could ever have known.

I continued to attend the special education unit until the summer of 2010, when, aged 16, I was the only pupil in my group to sit maths and English GCSE. When I opened my results that August, I was pleased to see I had passed both.

'I am not beaten yet,' I said to myself softly. 'No way.'

In the autumn, the teachers at the unit helped me to find a place on a hair and beauty course. It felt, at first, like the right fit. I was obsessed with make-up and hairstyles, after all. But as time went on, I struggled to concentrate. Though I loved learning beauty tips, they seemed superficial and unimportant – completely at odds with the worries that whirled around my head.

Jailed for just six years, I knew Chowdhury would serve only three, which meant he was due for release at any time. He might even be walking the streets now, looking for his next victim. Or looking for me. And all the other attackers, where were they? They could be driving past my college right now. They might be in the car park waiting for me. And Paul Waites. Where was he at, was he meeting another child outside Sainsbury's? Surely, he should be in prison too. I'd never told anyone that he had raped me. Never thought anyone would care.

It was impossible for me to focus in my lesson on skin types and tones, when I was worried about rapists tracking me down. So I left the course after a few weeks and my teachers instead helped me find a work experience placement at a local hospital. It would be my job, they explained, to organise and file paperwork in the offices there.

'Not the most exciting job,' they warned.

But I could already tell I was going to love it. Surrounded by jumbled piles of unallocated papers and files, I was in my element! I worked alone, methodically sorting and filing each set of papers. It was just like arranging my DVDs on the bookcase. Lost in my own world, I was amazed when my supervisor said:

'Sam, it's time to go home now. You've done a great job today, thank you.'

I shook my head.

'I just want to finish this last section,' I explained. 'Then I'll call it a day.'

I couldn't wait to go back the following morning. From the voluntary work in the offices, I was promoted to a paying role in the hospital pharmacy, where I packed drugs from a conveyor belt, loading them on to a robot and allocating a storage place. Controlled drugs, such as cancer medication, had to be allocated using a different system. Some drugs were obscure, or not properly labelled, so it was difficult to allocate them at all. But I relished the challenge. I loved planning, organising and tidying. Where my own life was upside down, my work environment was neatly under control, and I thrived on the chance to bring order and harmony to one area of my life, at least. My favourite mornings were arriving to find a pile of unassigned boxes that a colleague had obviously given up on the previous evening. I made it my mission to allocate them correctly, as well as finish my own schedule for the day. There was comfort in finding the correct home for each and every drug.

Not so easy to find that peace within myself.

17

ASIDE FROM my work, and my Friday nights with Granny Pat, I rarely went out, and I kept myself to myself. I stayed in touch with friends online only, turning down offers of nights out or shopping trips. A reclusive teenager, where possible I kept real-life at arm's length.

At 17, I learned to drive so that I could borrow my parents' car to get to work, or to visit Granny Pat. This felt much safer than public transport, where I was constantly checking the faces of the men sitting behind me and the men we drove past, in case I recognised them as my attackers. Even now, after five years, I was on high alert, and the process was exhausting. It never got any easier.

One evening, soon after I turned 18, I was idly scrolling online when I came across a message from someone named Steven Walker. He lived nearby and we had some mutual friends. We chatted, at first without any real enthusiasm on my part. I'd never had a boyfriend, and I wasn't looking for one either. The attacks had made me wary of all men. But it turned out we had lots in common.

Ste, as he was known, loved films just like me and he'd seen and rated all the ones I liked. He enjoyed cooking and eating out. Like me, he worked in a hospital, though he was a children's nurse. He was three years older than me and had just turned 21. The hours passed, the messages flew back and forth, and yet we still had lots to talk about.

'I've got to be up for work tomorrow,' I wrote. 'I need to sleep.'

'Me too,' he replied. 'I'll message you tomorrow.'

My phone pinged as I was cleaning my teeth early the next morning.

'How about I cook you dinner?' Ste wrote. 'Any night this week. A meal of your choice.'

My heart skipped a little as I typed:

'Tomorrow? And really, I'm not fussy. I'll eat whatever you cook.'

I was free every night, but I wanted to give him a chance to buy the ingredients, at least. All day at work, I smiled to myself as I loaded drugs on to the robot.

'I'm going out for dinner,' I said, as I skipped from one shelf to the next. 'I'm going on a date!'

I knew from the start that this was different in every way. It had snowed heavily that day and Ste messaged to say he would meet me at the bus stop. As the bus doors opened, I saw his face light up. I knew what he looked like already from his online photo: slim with short hair and glasses. He was wearing a leather jacket, jumper, jeans and boots, which were soon soaked in the deep snow.

'I'm really pleased you came,' he said shyly. 'I was starting to worry you might change your mind.'

As he opened his front door, he added, 'I haven't lived here long and it's the first time I've had my own place, so make allowances please,' he said. 'It needs lots of work.'

I could tell he was just as nervous as I was. All around the house, he had little figures of white tigers.

'I love them,' he told me bashfully.

And in his kitchen, he had a huge cookie jar filled with biscuits.

'I love those too!' he laughed.

Ste was geeky in an adorable way, and I fancied him right from that first night. He made me feel safe, too, there was something so reassuring and solid about him. He had cooked me his speciality: chicken biryani with bhajis, samosas and naans. It was a feast.

'You're a brilliant chef,' I said, finishing my last mouthful. 'That was delicious.'

Ste beamed.

'I hope that means you'll let me cook for you again,' he said.

I had no intention of falling in love and I didn't want a partner. Since the attacks, I was a hard nut to crack, and purposely so. But being with Ste was almost like being with an old friend – I felt I'd known him for years. And at the same time, there was still that thrill and buzz of a new relationship. It was the perfect, heady mix.

'See you tomorrow,' I smiled, and we shared our first kiss.

We began spending more and more time together, watching films, cooking dinners and enjoying long walks. I both feared and wanted a physical relationship with Ste, but I hadn't let anyone come near me since I was raped, and I knew intimacy would be difficult. How could I ever enjoy sex with him without reliving every appalling moment of the rapes? Yet in many ways, it was a good thing, to finally confront my trauma.

It was only through meeting Ste that I finally began to examine, and to admit to myself, what had really happened to me. As a child, I had not understood what rape was. Though the definition was explained to me, the emotional fallout was not. And even in counselling, we had focused more on coping from day to day; how to leave the house, how to get to sleep, how to survive the school run.

All I could cope with was to look to the future, without also examining the past. But now, with Ste, I was forced to confront it head on. The Man. The Boy. Paul Waites. Shakil Chowdhury. And all the other nameless cowards who had ruined me. Rape after rape after rape.

Each memory was like having my head shoved under ice-cold water, and every time it got harder and harder to swim back to the surface. Sometimes, I feared the ice would form over my head before I could reach the air, and I'd be trapped under there forever. I knew I had to give Ste some sort of explanation for my behaviour. It was only fair.

'Something happened to me when I was younger,' I told him. 'I'm sorry, but I have a few hang-ups about my body. I hope you can understand.'

That first time we slept together, I kept my T-shirt on. I just had to. That cruel comment about my belly stung just as much now as it had then. But Ste was so patient and understanding.

'You're beautiful,' he told me. 'But if you feel better keeping your T-shirt on in bed, I don't mind. Do whatever makes you feel comfortable.'

He loved me despite my issues, and maybe because of them. All I knew was, in his arms, I was happier than I had ever been.

The weeks passed and my inhibitions thawed a little. I could be myself with Ste because I felt so secure and loved.

'Let's go and get drunk,' he said one evening.

We went to Manchester's Hard Rock Café and, after trying every single cocktail, we somehow stumbled on to the bus and giggled the whole journey back. But nights like that were a rarity and neither of us were party animals. I had bypassed those carefree teenage years and, whilst I could never rewind, I didn't really want to, not with Ste in my life.

Besides, we were both busy working full-time, and most nights we were too tired to socialise. Ste was always happy to stay in and cook, and we'd rent a film or a boxset. We had fabulous curry nights, or he'd rustle up our favourites, sweet and sour pork for him, sweet and sour chicken for me.

Right from the start, I had referenced something bad happening in my past, and Ste had sensed it was serious. I was sketchy about my school days, vague when he asked about my friends, and overly anxious if he ever suggested going into Oldham town centre. Often, I hovered on the cusp of telling him the truth, but I did not know how to say the words out loud, even to myself. Where would I start? And what if he ran a mile? What if he decided I had too much baggage?

One night, curled up on the sofa after a curry, I gathered up every ounce of courage I had. I trusted Ste and I wanted him to trust me, too, and for that, he had to know the real me.

'When I was 12, I was raped by a gang of men,' I told him nervously. 'Many times.'

'Oh Sam,' he gasped, his eyes wide. 'I am so sorry. Please, let me hold you.'

I had worried he might reject me and walk away, but instead, he pulled me closer.

'Tell me about it if you can,' he said gently. 'Are they in prison?'

I shook my head.

'That's partly why I don't like going out,' I explained. 'One of them, the ringleader, served three years, the rest of them got away.'

'Three years?' he repeated, his jaw dropping. 'For raping a child?'

With my head down, I told him the full story. How I had been assaulted in the churchyard, but the police sent me away. How I was picked up by predators right outside the police station and raped in their car. How I was ensnared by another paedophile, who also raped me, before dumping me on the street. And how Chowdhury had promised to take me home in his taxi before driving me to his place and raping me many times and arranging for his friends to rape me too.

'I picked out the houses where I was raped. I showed the police the car. There were forensic tests. There must have been CCTV footage, especially inside and outside the police station. But they only convicted one man.'

Ste was outraged. Furious, on my behalf. And seeing it through his eyes, for the first time, I understood why.

'Why wasn't more done to catch these men?' he asked.

As I relived each attack, my shame crystallised into anger. I felt it had been played down, brushed under the carpet and waved away. Ste was right. These were horrific crimes. So why were they not taken more seriously?

'It's unbelievable that you were so badly failed, as such a young child,' Ste said, as the tears streamed down his cheeks. 'I'm so sorry, Sam.'

I hated to see him upset. Yet a small part of me felt bolstered by his support. He was on my side and he wanted to help me. Despite everything, he loved me still. And his reaction gave me the final push I needed to say:

'That's not all of it. I was groomed by a bloke online when I was 12. He made me do sexual stuff with him when we met. He raped me in a car park. It was horrible.'

Ste's head fell into his hands as if this was too much for him to bear.

'And is he in prison?' he asked.

'No,' I replied. 'I never reported it. I mentioned him when I was interviewed about the other rapes, but the police didn't seem to think he was important. I didn't want to bring it up again. There was only three weeks between the two sets of attacks, and I thought they would just think I was a slag. Waites is still out there, free to abuse other children, and it's all my fault.'

Ste pulled me closer to him.

'Don't ever say that again,' he said. 'It wasn't your fault. None of it was. When you feel ready, I want you to go to the police and report him. And I will be there with you. You don't need to go through this on your own, Sam. Not any more.'

I was so relieved, I burst into tears. I hadn't admitted, until now, how heavy my burden had weighed and how much I had been dreading sharing my secret.

'I thought you might leave me when you found out,' I admitted. 'I feel damaged and dirty. I thought you might want nothing more to do with me.'

'You're not damaged or dirty. You're incredibly brave,' he replied. 'You're a fighter.'

His words filled me with warmth and courage, and I realised I had been hoping, all these years, for this moment, for someone to champion me, to love me and to take my side. Ste was the saviour I never thought I needed. He and I began spending every day together, and the following March I moved in with him officially and we adopted two little Chihuahua dogs – first Lulu, followed by Mr Darcy.

I'd been living there a few weeks when, on my way home from work one day, I took a different bus with a slightly different route. As we reached a junction in the main road, I stared absent-mindedly out of the window and suddenly gasped in horror.

'No!' I muttered, closing my eyes as if I could somehow make the scene disappear.

I was just one stop from home, but to the right was the street where I had been raped by Chowdhury and his gang. I was living just a few minutes' walk away from the place where my life had been torn apart. Until now, I hadn't slotted together the geography of the two locations. Ste lived much closer to Chowdhury than I could ever have imagined.

When I got home, I told Ste.

'I had no idea, Sam, I'm sorry. But if you feel uncomfortable, we can move. I don't mind.'

'I can't stay here,' I said shakily. 'I'm sorry.'

I wanted to look for another place straight away. But when I thought it through over the next few days, it didn't make sense to run from the devil I knew, towards the devil I did not know. My attackers were quite possibly dotted like indelible stains all over Oldham. Moving away from one might just push me towards another. And I had no confirmation that Chowdhury still lived there. After his prison sentence, he might well have moved away.

'No, we'll stay,' I said to Ste. 'I feel safe with you here.'

That April, we booked a caravan holiday in North Wales, and one night, at a cabaret, I sent a jokey text to Ste:

'Marry me!'

The following afternoon, under grey, chilly skies and the threat of rain, Ste announced we should go to the beach.

'The forecast isn't good,' I warned him. 'Should we maybe go another day?'

But Ste was strangely agitated, insisting we needed to go to the beach immediately.

'I'd like to paddle in the sea,' he said. 'We'll be fine if we keep our coats on.'

Bemused, I agreed, and together we paddled along the shoreline, with our coats zipped up and our jeans rolled to our knees. Ste still seemed distracted and on edge, and he had one hand in his pocket at all times.

'What's the matter?' I asked him. 'You've been acting weirdly all day.'

He smiled shyly, and from his pocket, he produced a small ring box and flipped it open. I saw a diamond glinting in the weak sunlight and my heart leapt.

'Sam, please marry me,' he said, dropping to his knee in the water, soaking his jeans and his coat sleeves.

'Yes!' I yelled, throwing my arms around him. 'Yes, of course!'

We kissed in the sea as he pushed a traditional white gold diamante ring on to my finger. We were both soaked and cold and covered in sand. But it didn't matter one bit. For the first time, my life had purpose, hope and love.

My life had Ste.

18

BACK AT home, I began to think about reporting Paul Waites to the police. In one area of my life, I was blissfully happy, deeply in love and engaged to be married. I had also been offered a new job as a mobile carer, and I couldn't wait to get started. But the spectre of the abuse hung about me like cobwebs. It preyed on my mind, in particular that Waites was free to abuse other young girls and I had a growing sense of a duty to speak out. With Ste's support, I told myself I no longer cared what the police thought of me. I did not care how they judged me. The important thing was to get Waites off the streets.

'I think I'm ready,' I said to Ste.

'You're doing the right thing,' he replied.

He flipped open his laptop and typed 'Paul Waites' into the search engine. I peered over his shoulder, not expecting anything to show up. But to my alarm, there he was, right in front of me. The image sent a shudder right through me. Horribly, Waites was posing on a modelling website, with his name and age listed alongside a creepy head shot, in which he was staring moodily into the camera in much the same way he had in the photo he'd sent to me, so long ago.

'That's him,' I shivered as his photo flashed on to the screen 'Oh God, that's him.'

Ste took a screenshot.

'Do you remember anything else about him?' he asked, noting down the website details. 'An address or a phone number?'

Paul Waites had never given me his address. I only knew that he lived in Stockport, though I realised now that was probably a lie. But to my surprise, his phone number tripped easily off my tongue and I repeated it easily, all those years later. My heart stuttered as Ste punched the numbers into his mobile and pressed dial. As the call rang out, my whole body tensed.

'Hello?' said a man's voice through the speakerphone, and immediately I collapsed with relief.

'It's not him,' I mouthed to Ste.

It turned out the number now belonged to someone else, and in a way, I was pleased. I wasn't sure I could bear to hear Waites speak. Ste spent the whole evening researching online and then he rang the police station to make an appointment for the following week.

'What if they don't believe me?' I fretted. 'What if they send me away, just like they did when I was 12 years old?'

'This is different,' Ste said, efficiently collating all his information into a file on his laptop. 'I'm with you. I won't let them fail you again, Sam. I promise.'

After years of feeling as though I was drowning, Ste's support was like a buoy, keeping me afloat. He made everything seem reasonable and possible.

An officer came to see us and when I explained I wanted to report a historical sexual attack, he replied:

'How do you expect me to walk into a man's home when he could have a wife and children by now?'

Suddenly I felt sick with guilt, as though this was my fault for ruining Waites' life. But Ste said angrily:

'If he has a wife and family then it's all the more important you walk into his house. This man is dangerous.'

The officer took more details and arranged for me to go into the station to give a video interview. After arriving, we spoke briefly with an officer before Ste was asked to wait in another area.

'Samantha will be here a while, so you might want to go home and come back?' the officer suggested.

'No,' Ste replied loyally. 'I'll be right here waiting for her.'

I was shown into a small room, which was completely green. Too green, I said to myself, with a critical eye, using my usual deflection tactic of focusing on the minutiae. There was a two-seater, plastic-leather green sofa and large green tiles on the walls that reminded me of the wall tiles in the toilets near Oldham market, where I'd changed out of my school uniform to go drinking with my pals. It took all my strength not to be dragged down a rabbit hole of grim reminders.

'No, Sam,' I said to myself firmly. 'Not today.'

The female officer was initially confused as I tried to explain that three weeks prior to the rapes by the gang, I had also been attacked by Paul Waites.

'So this was a separate incident, which you didn't report at the time?' she asked.

'That's right,' I mumbled, my head down.

My cheeks flamed with humiliation, and I felt sure she was judging me, wondering how on earth one girl could be attacked so many times and by so many people. Did she even believe me? My skin prickled with paranoia as I remembered my social worker's damning verdict: 'It is hard to know if Sam is telling the truth.'

What if the police thought that too?

'Tell me about Paul Waites,' she said.

I did my best, but casting my mind back to those three meetings on the Sainsbury's car park was painful and hard. I had blocked out so much, buried it so deeply that it was impossible now to simply spring it back to the surface on demand. I had to recount, too, all the calls, messages, pictures, and expert manipulation in between. He had reeled me in like a small and fragile fish, and at the last minute he had ripped my throat out with the hook.

'If you remember anything else, please let us know,' the officer said. 'We'll be in touch.'

A few weeks later, I was called back to the station to the VIPER (Video Identification Parades Electronic Recording) suite. As always, Ste came with me, his hand in mine, his unconditional support more valuable than he could ever have known. Sitting in front of the screen, I suddenly shuddered violently as Paul Waites' face flashed in front of me.

'That's him,' I said instantly. 'Number 5. That's him.'

Even when he was on a screen and could not hurt me, he still terrified me. For a few moments, I was plugged back into the electrifying horror, and I felt his hands gripping my head and forcing it down. I watched, retching, as he cleaned himself with his towel and offered me nothing.

Was this what I was worth?

I was given an appointment for a second video interview, and this time when I returned, the room had been refurbished, with a dark two-seater sofa and striped cushions. It looked much friendlier. As always, Ste was waiting for me outside, refusing to leave the station without me. An officer introduced herself and pushed copies of news reports across the small table towards me. The headline, from a paper in West Yorkshire, jumped out and smacked me.

Sex trap teacher is jailed.

And there it was, neatly summarised in the newspaper. A myriad of horrors. One blistering blow after another. Paul Waites was already in prison for attacking someone else. He was a former primary school teacher and had previously worked with young children. When he attacked me, he'd been 34 years old, almost double what he had claimed. The revelations took my breath away, each one rippling through me like an aftershock of a deadly explosion.

'He's done it before. He's done it before,' I said to myself. 'I was not the first.'

But on one level, I'd always known that. I knew he was a danger. His methods were sickeningly slick and his exploitation of me had been confident and well rehearsed. Of course I was not the only one. And it was so much more important now to see this through and ensure he never left his prison cell. I was doing this not just for me but for the other children, too. Maybe there were some victims who had never been able to speak out. I had a duty to be their voice.

'He's done it before,' I told Ste, as we left the station. 'I feel sick at the thought of it.'

Now, it seemed even worse that he had abused other children, as well as me, because I did not feel I mattered as much. I felt my own suffering was less important. Later, Ste and I worked out that Waites was due for release from prison, so the timing of my complaint was perfect. Hopefully, I could make sure he was locked up again for a long time. The stress of the interview process, raking over my old scars, made me ill and I turned to Hayley for more counselling. The abuse was dominating our lives and I hoped that, at least, this might be the end of the police process. But then I was called back for yet another recorded interview. Just as before, Ste came with me to wait, and I was shown into the little room that I now knew so well. I had no idea why the police needed to speak to me yet again. But this time, a different officer introduced herself, before asking if I remembered referencing Paul Waites in my interview in 2006, after the rape by the gangs.

'No,' I replied. 'I don't remember that. To be honest, I remember nothing from that interview except that I was desperate to have a bath. I really wanted to wash myself and I couldn't concentrate on anything else except how horrible I felt.'

The officer pursed her lips and began to read out a transcript from my interview in 2006, where I had described calling Paul Waites after that first assault in the churchyard.

'Yes,' I nodded, as the memory flooded back. 'I did say that.'

'And,' she said. 'You said that your mum doesn't like you seeing him and that he's a really good mate of yours and he's there for you. Do you remember saying that?'

'No, no,' I replied.

'Do you remember why you would say that, what your reason was for saying that, because if what we're saying now is that he subjected you to sexual offences, then why would you say that?'

I stared at her in disbelief. I suddenly felt as if I was under investigation, as though she was challenging me and my version of events. As though I was the one in the wrong. My throat felt blocked, as though I'd swallowed a pebble.

'Because I was a kid?' I suggested.

'What do you mean, you were a kid?' she said.

'I was a kid, just gang-raped, so it was more important,' I muttered, spitting out each word like it was a piece of grit from between my teeth.

But she wasn't done with me.

'Why didn't you say anything about him?' she pressed. 'You just said he was a good friend and nothing else had happened… From what you're saying now, you've been orally raped by him sometime before you were gang-raped.'

If I had felt dirty and worthless at the time of the attacks, then I felt it doubly now. I had turned to the police for help, but I felt the officer was peering at me like I was a small grub, like I belonged under her shoe and not here in this room.

'Cos I had enough to worry about at the time,' I mumbled.

'Okay. Can you just explain that for me?' she said.

The answers screamed inside my head:

I didn't tell the police about Paul Waites because I had no headspace! I didn't tell them because I was battered, bruised and broken. Because I had just been raped over and over by many different men. Because I was a confused and terrified little girl! Because I was a victim. Because I thought it was my fault. Because I was worried I would be in trouble. Because…

Instead, I stared at her and said nothing. The silence between us stretched tight like a band. Any moment, it might snap completely. Was I on trial here? Was I being held to account in a way that my attackers, ironically, never had been? And bubbling in the back of my mind was a far more serious concern. As a vulnerable 12-year-old, I had told police officers, who were investigating multiple rapes against me, that I was in touch with an 18-year-old male online who my mother wouldn't approve of. I had told them I'd met him in person. Yet they had done nothing. It wasn't investigated or even explored further, at that time or at any other. Instead of grilling me about my decision to stay silent, surely this officer should have been apologising to me and explaining why the police hadn't looked into Paul Waites in 2006? She shuffled her papers and tried a different tack.

'What were your feelings towards him like at that time?'

I shrugged. I couldn't remember having feelings. I didn't even remember feeling human. But then I did remember feeling I wanted not to be alive, not to wake every day being crushed by a crippling mix of shame, guilt, and self-loathing. I said none of that. I sat quietly, shrinking under her gaze, and feeling I was under suspicion, feeling I was being called out as a liar and a slut. She even referenced the 'relationship' between Paul Waites and me, asking: 'Why did that relationship stop?'

She seemed to be saying that, aged 12, I had been old enough to have a relationship. The choice of terminology left me reeling and nauseous.

There was no relationship! I was 12 years old! I was groomed and raped. I was damaged and destroyed!

But again, I said nothing.

Thankfully, she had no more questions, and so I gathered my bag and jacket and left with my head down. It had taken every ounce of courage I had to report Paul Waites to the police. But as Ste and I walked out into the Oldham rain, I felt I had made a huge mistake.

19

WHEN WE got home, Ste sensed I was upset about something more than the case itself.

'The officer spoke to me as though it was my fault that I hadn't reported Paul Waites earlier,' I wept. 'Or perhaps she thought I wasn't telling the truth, because when I was 12, I had described him as a mate. I just don't think they believe me, Ste. I wish I'd never reported it.'

Ste was aghast.

'We need to make a complaint about this,' he said, already typing furiously on his laptop. 'The more I look into your case, the more horrified I become. I think the whole thing needs to be re-examined. The system needs to change, for you and for all other survivors, Sam.'

It felt like an impossible challenge, but as I dried my eyes, I was swept along, in that moment, by his passion and enthusiasm. How could I not be when it was driven by his love for me? He was a young man who wanted to change the world, and it was all for me. He could have been plucked out of one of the Disney fairytales I'd loved so much as a child – a knight in shining armour, a handsome, dazzling prince on horseback. Fate had dealt me a cruel hand in life so far. But meeting Ste was a blessing I could only ever have dreamed of.

'Yes,' I agreed. 'You're right. It's not a fair system.'

A few weeks later, Waites was charged with sexual assault and rape. The prospect of another court hearing did not scare me as much this time, because I had Ste by my side. Protective and kind, he was with me every step of the way. He had, he confessed, been through his own trauma as a child, and perhaps that made him especially empathetic to mine.

'We need a name for our campaign,' Ste said thoughtfully, as he flicked through files on his laptop. 'We want people to sit up and take notice of us.'

Later, I was dozing off in front of the TV, when he suddenly yelled.

'I've got the campaign title! "You have not defeated me"! What do you think, Sam? It shows you've still got fight in you. It sends a message to everyone who has let you down, your attackers, the social workers, the police and the justice system.'

'I love it,' I beamed, throwing my arms around him.

Trust Ste to have found the perfect way to express how I felt. That weekend, I got a tattoo of the campaign name on my arm.

You have not defeated me

'A lasting reminder,' I smiled as I rolled up my sleeve to show him.

'But what if the campaign fails? What if it amounts to nothing? What if I let you down?' he frowned.

'That's not what this is about,' I replied, loving him for his vulnerability. 'It can never be a failure, because I have you on my side. Whatever happens, it was worth it.'

Ste already had a mini manifesto written out on his laptop. Our campaign was aimed at raising awareness both of sexual crimes against children and of the failure of public bodies to react and investigate. Ste launched a Facebook page, under the campaign name, and invited local media to join.

'You should write an open letter, to the perpetrators,' he suggested. 'Tell them how you feel and how they destroyed your life, but how you will continue fighting. People need to understand how much you have suffered. It's a powerful message, but this is what we need.'

His eyes shone with such belief and intensity that it was contagious. A few months earlier, I couldn't have shared my thoughts with anyone, and now I was preparing to tell the whole world how I felt. That was the 'Ste-effect': he made me feel I could achieve anything – that I had worth, at last. Nevertheless, it was not an easy letter to write, and as my emotions spilled on to the paper, my tears did too. I called it, 'Letter to a Monster' and I wrote:

You have not defeated me. For years I served your sentence with you, and longer. I could not look at my body and hated to recognise myself because I reminded myself of you. You beat me, bit me, mocked me and made me hate myself so much I wanted to die, and at first, I thought I deserved it. But our long-term relationship is over, you do not deserve me anymore. I will experience all my life has to offer and achieve as much as I can in this lifetime, but for me not for you. I am free from the prison you built for me, and I will fight with every breath in my body to stop people like you hurting any other children. You will live with the shame of your crimes, and if I ever get the opportunity to have you serve the time you really deserved, then believe me, you will serve it.

Ste added a link to an E-petition, which aimed to see the notion of 'ostensible consent' abolished in relation to cases with young victims. Current laws mean children under 13 cannot legally give consent to sexual acts. But the notion of ostensible consent – an offender's 'perception' that the victim has consented – can be used in court as a mitigating factor. We wanted to change that.

'Ready?' he asked, and I nodded.

With a click, he uploaded my letter and, in that moment, our campaign went live. My secret was out. I went to bed consumed with both pride and fear. By the next morning, our phones were ringing and pinging and the Facebook page was jumping with likes and comments. I was flabbergasted. In truth, I hadn't really expected anyone to be that interested. But I hadn't reckoned on Ste's expert marketing techniques. Our local paper, the *Oldham Chronicle*, asked if they could run our story.

'That would be brilliant,' I said.

The reporter explained I would have to sign away my automatic right to anonymity, as a victim of a sexual offence.

'I understand,' I replied. 'And yes, I want my voice to be heard. I've been silent for far too long and that's exactly what the perpetrators want. It's time to fight back.'

After our campaign featured on the front page of the local paper, we were contacted by national media, newspapers, radio and television.

'We're speaking out against the paedophiles but also against the system which fails to bring them to justice,' Ste said.

He knew exactly what to say and how to say it, and I was much more comfortable letting him be the mouthpiece whilst I hovered in the shadows in the background. Ste had an in-built moral compass, a social conscience that gave him a burning desire to put wrongs right. It was a basic premise, but he did it with such intelligence, compassion and skill. He was the cleverest man I'd ever met, and I was in awe of him. And he seemed to take it all in his stride too.

'We have BBC tomorrow morning, followed by Channel 4 and then an interview with the Daily Mirror,' he said, ticking off his checklist on his laptop. 'It's all going to plan.'

For me, it was way off plan, I hadn't expected any of this, but it was marvellous all the same. I was on a natural high. For so many years, I'd had no voice. I'd been made to feel like I didn't matter, not only by my abusers but by the social workers, the police and the courts who were supposed to protect me. Ste was determined to change all of that.

As well as the media attention, my inbox was overflowing with messages from other survivors and their families; girls like me who had been abused twice – firstly by their attackers and then by the system.

'I have felt so lonely all these years.'

'I kept quiet because I thought it was my fault. I thought everyone would blame me because I kept going back to meet him.'

'I feel so ashamed. I've not even told my family the whole truth.'

Their words resonated right through me. They could have

been my own. But alongside the show of love and support were the trolls and the haters who sent me vile messages.

'Slut! You were asking for it!'

'Girls like you are the problem, not the men!'

'Your own fault for being out late drinking and getting in that taxi!'

Again, those words struck a chord because they could have been my own. Nobody could be crueller to me than I had been to myself. There was so much ignorance and mis-information surrounding grooming. I received well-meaning messages to say I was not a victim of grooming because it hadn't taken place in a takeaway. Another said I hadn't been groomed because it had happened over a 24-hour period, and a longer timescale was needed. Other messages laid the blame for the grooming epidemic on men of Pakistani heritage.

'The ringleader when I was gang-raped was Bangladeshi,' I said. 'This is not a race issue.'

It was exhausting, arguing against other people's preju-dices and explaining away their misconceptions. Immersing myself in their problems, I was aware I was neglecting my own. But it was a small price to pay, Ste reminded me, for the success of the campaign. Keen to capitalise on our publicity, he wrote to the Prime Minister, David Cameron, on my behalf, to ask for a public inquiry into child sexual exploita-tion (CSE). I wasn't holding out for a reply, but he wrote back quite quickly, and his response was far more encouraging than either of us could have hoped for. I was invited to take part in an Inquiry into localised child grooming, headed by Keith Vaz, chairman of the Home Affairs Select Committee. As I read the information from Mr Vaz, I raised my eyebrows in awe. There were many famous names and agencies involved: Esther Rantzen, NSPCC, Barnardo's, various police forces and councils, the serious organised crime agency, domestic abuse support groups – and me! It was at once terrifying and exhilarating.

'I'll be with you,' Ste promised. 'Don't worry about that. You're not on your own Sam, not any longer.'

I nodded and squeezed his hand.

'I know,' I replied.

But though I smiled, I had the briefest sensation that I was hopping aboard something that was travelling slightly too fast. Still, I pushed the feeling aside. This was no time to have second thoughts. I was asked, first of all, to give evidence in writing, and Ste helped me to organise my thoughts. He was now studying law part-time and, motivated by his enthusiasm for my case, was moving away from nursing and towards a job in the legal profession. In our evidence, we wrote:

Young people and children face an incredible amount of prejudice in the court system and public services are not properly equipped nor properly accountable for the prevention, detection and management of child sexual exploitation… This is a large-scale problem, and the current attitude seems to be that it is okay for children to be sexually abused and exploited, public confidence is low and our current way of dealing with this problem is clearly ineffective, it is time for change, it's time for this to end.

We were then invited to travel to Westminster to meet Keith Vaz in person, to explain how and why the system had failed me personally. We had so many points of concern, right across all the agencies. I hardly knew where to start. But again, Ste stepped in and prepared a bulletpoint list of our major grievances.

Hurrying off the train at Euston station, his hand in mine, I again had that exhilarating sensation of being able to achieve anything at all. Mr Vaz was warm and friendly and seemed genuinely concerned by what I had been through.

'You've been a major help, Samantha,' he said.

Not long after, I got a letter from the Deputy Children's Commissioner, Sue Berelowitz, requesting a meeting.

'Another trip to London!' I said, my excitement streaked with worry.

Even though I'd already met Keith Vaz, it was still an over-facing, and I barely slept the night before our trip. At 5am the next morning, as we were rushing out for the train, Ste bent to fasten his shoes, and his suit trousers ripped loudly across his bum. All tension gone, I dissolved into giggles as he crossly changed into a pair of black jeans.

'It looks very unprofessional,' he grumbled. 'But there's no time to find another pair of trousers.'

Then, when we arrived at Westminster, we were told that Ste had to remain in a waiting room and I met with Ms Berelowitz on my own. Though I'd rather have had him with me, it at least spared his blushes in his jeans. When the Keith Vaz report was published, my case was described as: *'one of the most serious examples of rape and sexual exploitation of children in the United Kingdom over the past decade.'*

The claim sent a cold chill right through me. Yet it also quashed my doubts over whether speaking out was the right thing to do. I had been given a platform, and I owed it to all children to use it well.

The interest in our campaign intensified, and our lives became a whirlwind of meetings and interviews. I met Ed Miliband, the leader of the Labour Party, and Andy Burnham, the mayor of Greater Manchester. I was also introduced to various members of Oldham Council and Greater Manchester Police. It was mind-boggling. Not so long ago, I'd been a child who nobody wanted to listen to. Now, everyone wanted to speak to me, or at least they wanted to be seen to want to speak to me.

'Damage limitation,' Ste said wisely. 'Some of these people will know that the investigation into your attackers was flawed and now they're panicking. They want to make sure they're on the right side of the argument.'

No matter how many dignitaries I met, I found each meeting stressful, and I couldn't have got through those occasions on my own. Ste was my guardian, overseeing all communications and deflecting all difficult questions. I needed him as a kind of buffer between me and the outside world. I felt so confident with him on my side that I stopped taking my ADHD and autism medication. It was a big decision, but I was used to making these by now. Without my prescribed safety blanket, I felt suddenly raw and edgy. But I was also thinking clearly and logically, for the first time in around six years. There was no longer a screen between me and other people. I was naturally blunter and more straight-talking and, in some interviews, I noticed people wincing or frowning at my frankness. Others, I think, welcomed my honesty. I had lost myself after the attacks and this was the real me, emerging like a butterfly from a chrysalis. It was not an exaggeration to say that this felt like a second chance at life.

Running parallel to his work in the media and with the authorities, Ste was frantically busy, night after night, digging into the details surrounding the attack in October 2006. I had never, to my memory, had a letter informing me that Shakil Chowdhury was free. But with only a six-year jail sentence, I assumed he was out on licence somewhere. After weeks of research, Ste announced he had found the hostel in Manchester where Chowdhury was living.

'How on earth did you do that?' I asked.

'It wasn't easy,' he admitted. 'I made lots of phone calls. It was a process of elimination too. I'm going to drive over there, just to be sure. I understand if you don't want to come, Sam.'

But he had a lit a fire within me and there was no way I wanted to be left behind.

'Of course I want to come!' I replied. 'Let's go now!'

On the journey there, I played out scenes in my head where I would confront Chowdhury on the street, just as he was leaving his hostel. In one daydream, I addressed him calmly, asking why he had raped me and why he had protected the other gang members. In another fantasy, I saw myself running into the hostel and dragging him out of his room. The pent-up anger and grief that had festered within me since I was 12 years old now bubbled to the surface. Like a pot simmering quietly on a stove for years, I was about to boil over.

'This is your chance,' I told myself. 'Take it.'

After a half-hour's drive, Ste turned into a side road.

'This is it. This is his street.'

We parked and, to my dismay, I spotted a school further down the same road.

'How could they house him so close to a school?' I asked, choking on my words. 'How could they let him live near children?'

I lifted my head as I zipped up my coat, and there, on the pavement just yards away, was Chowdhury. This was exactly as I had imagined it, him walking towards me, just metres away. I could barely believe it was happening and yet there he was, the human embodiment of evil, staring straight at me. I have no idea if he recognised me, but I would have known him anywhere. The cold dark eyes, the defiant lift of his chin. The casual swagger, a cigarette dangling from one hand, the other in his pocket.

There is no way you're 12 years old!

But it was there that the scene stopped. I did not, as I had fantasised, calmly confront him, nor did I scream and shout. I did not run to attack him or to remonstrate with him. In that heartbreaking moment, I was a little girl again, 12 years old, vulnerable and scared out of my wits. Standing still in the middle of the pavement, I began to tremble so violently that Ste immediately worked out what was going on.

'Shakil Chowdhury?' he called.

Chowdhury was not so brave when confronted with another man. Without replying, he ran back into the hostel and pressed a panic alarm. Whilst Ste was helping me to get my breath back at the side of the road, a police car screamed to a halt outside the hostel.

'We haven't done anything,' Ste explained. 'We didn't even speak to him.'

Back in the car, I held my head in my hands. Images from that night scuttled, like rodents, around my head. The Bumbly Bee lampshade. The towels on the pillow. The men laughing as they took turns to rape me.

'You must wash yourself because I like cleanliness.'

'It looks like Chowdhury is very well protected,' said Ste, as he started the engine. 'What a shame the police weren't quite so keen to help you after him and his mates raped you.'

20

THE TRIP to see Chowdhury had shaken me, but it had also given me purpose and I knew I had to act on the information, because he was living so near to young children. I contacted my MP, Debbie Abrahams, to ask why he had not been deported after serving his sentence. From the trial reports, we knew Chowdhury was of Bangladesh origin but had been granted British citizenship in 2004, just two years before he attacked me. My belief was that this ought to have been revoked after the attacks.

'This man is a danger,' I wrote. 'Why is he allowed to live here?'

My argument had nothing whatsoever to do with race. My attackers had all been of Asian heritage. But there were also white grooming gangs. This was not a race issue. However, in Chowdhury's case, it was surely wrong not to deport him for the safety of other children. Ms Abrahams was fully supportive. But when we then wrote to the Home Office, they would not consider my plea. They didn't give me a reason, or even an alternative plan to ensure society was safe from Chowdhury. It felt as though the system was closing ranks around him, helping him, and not me. In years before, a response like this from the authorities would have rattled me. But now, it only spurred me on to keep fighting. And Ste, as usual, was ready to launch the next chapter of our battle.

I had been troubled ever since the attacks by the notion that the house where I was gang-raped had been set up as a lair to trap children. The condoms in the child's bedroom, the towels on the pillows, the entitled behaviour of the attackers… everything made me think it had happened before.

'We need evidence to show that these men were serial offenders,' Ste said. 'So, we should go to the street ourselves. We could knock on doors, one by one, and ask people what they know.'

It seemed at once an obvious suggestion, yet also completely insane.

'I can't go back there,' I stuttered. 'I can't do it. I can't walk down his street.'

Ste took my hands in his.

'*We* are going back there,' he reminded me. 'Not you, not I, not me. *We* and *us*. It might do you good, Sam, to confront this. Don't let them control you. You have nothing at all to be scared of on that street. You can do it.'

If Ste had announced he wanted me to climb Everest, I would probably have believed I could manage it somehow. I was carried along on a wave of something almost euphoric. I was taking back control of my life and I was smashing open all the doors that had been slammed in my face, time after time, year after year.

'Okay,' I said nervously. 'I'll give it a go.'

It was a week or so before our shifts at work allowed us a few hours of daylight to go to the street. I didn't want to turn up in the dark; I was worried about my own safety and about upsetting local residents too. I felt they were more likely to talk to us in daylight.

When the afternoon finally came around, I was eaten up with a cocktail of fear, trepidation and excitement. On our walk there, Ste ran through our lists of questions. He'd brought us a clipboard each to make us seem more official.

'Got it,' I said nervously. 'I understand what I need to do.'

But as we turned into the street, my whole body seemed to liquefy. I clung on to Ste, wishing I could somehow disappear into his leather jacket. This was it. This was the place. The front door of Chowdhury's home had been changed, or maybe it had just been painted. But the house was unmistakeably the same. The windows glared at me. The walls exuded evil. I wondered if the Bumbly Bee lampshade still hung upstairs. Unable to move, I was pinned to the pavement by memories of the past, revisiting a horror I was so desperate to forget.

'Do you want to do it another day?' Ste asked kindly.

'No,' I replied, shaking my head firmly. 'I have to do this.'

My heart was banging against my ribs as I knocked on the first door. Anti-climatically, there was no response. At the second door, a man opened it an inch and snapped: 'Not interested!'

I hadn't even opened my mouth, and I wondered whether the clipboard had made him think I was doing some sort of survey. On the other side of the street, Ste evidently felt the same, because I spotted his clipboard abandoned on a garden wall. He was leaning on a doorway and was deep in conversation with a middle-aged couple. At the third house, an elderly lady answered.

'I wondered if you knew about the attacks in 2006 at the house a few doors down?' I asked her. 'I'm trying to find out what kind of people lived there.'

'Oh,' she shuddered. 'I was so glad when he was arrested. There was a constant stream of taxis and young girls, to and from that house. Lots of noise, all hours of the day and night and it stopped me sleeping sometimes.

'I complained to the council, but nothing was done. It's much more peaceful here now. I'm so relieved he went to prison.'

I'd always known it. But hearing her say it out loud set my teeth on edge.

A constant stream of taxis and young girls...

How many other girls had suffered there, as I had? Another householder told me the same story: how he had complained about the late-night comings and goings and how he was particularly concerned about the age of the girls he had seen there.

'Young girls with middle-aged men,' he told me bluntly. 'It wasn't right.'

When I met up with Ste at the bottom of the street, he had heard similar reports. Most people, admittedly, didn't want to speak to us. But when they did, their stories were distressing.

'Before we leave, let's speak to the people in nearby streets as well,' said Ste.

'Oh yes,' said a lady. 'I know the man you mean. I was once walking down that street and I heard a young girl screaming in his house. I was so frightened, I didn't know what to do. He was a very scary man.'

'Did you not call the police?' I pressed.

She shook her head.

'I was very afraid,' she said, in a whisper. 'I'm sorry.'

I was in tears as she closed her door. My heart went out to that little girl and all the others too. She might even have been describing me, but I didn't remember screaming when Chowdhury raped me. I was neither brave nor foolish enough to protest that night.

'That poor girl,' I said to Ste, as we turned for home.

'Yes, and poor you,' he replied. 'If the authorities had listened to these residents, to their complaints about the taxis and the noise, the men might have been arrested. If they'd taken all this seriously, Sam, those animals might have been off the streets, and you might never have been attacked in the first place.'

The realisation didn't make me as sad or as angry as it might once have done, because now I was grasping on to something positive; change for the future.

Ste and I returned to the streets the following week, and listened to more similar accounts, enough to build up a pattern of paedophile activity over the years. When we got home, Ste collated our results and then he called Greater Manchester Police.

Naively, I was expecting them to thank us for our help and ask us for the details of what we had learned. Instead, two officers came to the house and told us, in no uncertain terms, to stop meddling.

'You're not doing any good,' said one. 'You're not breaking any laws, so we can't order you to stay away from that street. But we would rather you didn't go back.'

I was speechless. The police had made so many mistakes in the way my case had been handled. And now, instead of learning from those, they were simply making more.

21

STE WAS not, luckily, the sort of man who was easily discouraged. Now Greater Manchester Police (GMP) had made it clear they were not interested in our work on Chowdhury's former street, he filed a complaint and then he switched his attentions elsewhere. He contacted Ann Coffey, the MP for Stockport, who was the chair of the all-party parliamentary group for runaway and missing children and adults. Ms Coffey was working to show how internet providers were not doing enough to protect children, and how more safety measures were needed.

'There are no safety measures at all!' I told her. 'I was groomed online when I was 12 years old and there were no checks. In fact, I bet nothing has changed even now.'

Ste and I came up with a plan to join the same website where Paul Waites had groomed me. Posing as children, our aim was to prove the point that this site and others like it needed stricter regulation. First of all, with Ste's support, I approached the administrators of the website to let them know what I was planning. I also assured them that all conversations would be recorded. For me, having been trapped in the murky world of exploitation, transparency was of paramount importance. I made an account and logged on that same afternoon, just around the time children everywhere were coming home from school. Even though I was now an adult, even though I knew this was all a sham, I felt physically sick as the first message flashed up on my screen.

'Hi gorgeous girl.'

'Hiya, I'm Sam, 13 years old,' I wrote.

'I'm 18,' he replied.

More than once, I made it clear that I was a child. But the man did not seem to mind, or rather, that was precisely what he was looking for. He started to masturbate and began giving me instructions. Revolted, I ordered him to stop and informed him that I was in fact a 20-year-old woman.

'I will be handing my recording to the police,' I wrote. 'But first I will give you the option to hand yourself in. If you don't, I'll do it for you.'

By the end of the night, my inbox was inundated with messages from men requesting a private conversation. My stomach roiled in disgust. Even after my own experiences, I had not expected it to be this easy, or for the predators to be quite so blatant and prolific. The next night, bracing myself, I made a new account and started all over again. Within moments, I had an approach.

'I'm going to the police,' I told him. 'Everything is recorded.'

Over the next couple of nights, I made contact with 14 paedophiles. Several of the men sent their phone numbers and asked if they could call me. I could not bear to speak to them, but Ste, as usual, was ready with a solution, and he used a voice distortion machine to make him sound like a young girl. Once the men confirmed they understood they were talking to a 13-year-old girl and the conversation became sexual, he switched the machine off and informed them they had been recorded.

There was no satisfaction, no feeling of victory, as I deleted my account. I felt queasy and unclean, as though they had infected me by association. I could not face joining any more websites, but our research proved everything we had feared and more. There was a thick soup of predators swirling around on the internet, just waiting for young victims. It was depressing to think that so many twisted individuals actually existed. Ste and I handed our recordings to GMP who, I was not by now surprised, appeared irritated by our efforts.

'We would like you to back off,' they said.

'Why?' Ste challenged them. 'Why should we? What law are we breaking?'

The officers admitted we were not breaking any laws and that they could only advise – and not order – us to stop.

'We're trying to make a point,' Ste told them. 'Grooming children online is all too easy and happens all too often. It has to stop. If these websites were properly policed, there would be no need for us to do this.'

In July 2014, two of the paedophiles who had approached me appeared at Manchester's Minshull Street Crown Court, the same court where Shakil Chowdhury had been convicted. Lee Barton, 47, from Doncaster, and Darren Bates, 36, from Warrington, had both earlier admitted attempting to incite a child to engage in sexual activity. Barton was jailed for 21 months. Bates was given a 15-month jail term suspended for 18 months.

The court heard that Ste and I had set up false usernames on a website and that within minutes of posing as a 13-year-old girl, we were inundated by attempts at grooming by men. Barton made contact, claiming to be 18, requesting a private conversation and he even supplied his mobile phone number.

Philip Curran, prosecuting, told the court: 'The defendant asked for a picture and whether she was on her own, where her mother and father were, what time they finished work and if she wanted him to come round.'

Bates contacted another false username and asked me, posing as a 13-year-old child, to carry out an indecent act. A recording of the call was then passed to police.

At a separate hearing, Philip Moule, 66, of Basildon, Essex, pleaded guilty to attempting to arrange or facilitate the commission of a child sex offence and attempting to cause a child to watch an image of sexual activity. He was sentenced to a three-year community order.

After the sentencings, Det Sgt John Coleman, of GMP, said: 'While we have a number of convictions here today, there is always a danger that this type of vigilante-style activity could impact negatively on any future court proceedings, which no doubt goes against their initial intention.

'We strongly encourage people not to take the law into their own hands and to contact the police at the earliest possible time to enable us to look into it professionally.'

Steven was furious at the negative reporting of the case.

We were described by the police and in the media as 'vigilantes' and we felt they were accusing us, when in fact we had helped to expose and convict three dangerous paedophiles. The language and narrative around child grooming was just as backward as it had been in 2006, and I felt as though nothing had changed.

GMP later issued an apology and some of the news articles were withdrawn. But the culture remained the same, and for me, the victory was a hollow one.

22

IN THAT same summer of 2014, Ste and I set a date for our wedding. He suggested we should choose the closest date possible to the gang rapes, so that the anniversary of the attacks now became the anniversary of our wedding; the worst possible memory replaced by the very best.

'That's a lovely idea,' I said. 'As long as you don't mind.'

'Why would I mind?' Ste replied. 'We're a team.'

Despite his assurances, I couldn't help feeling the attacks were overshadowing our lives and dictating everything we did. For years, I had locked myself away and nobody had even mentioned the rapes. It had felt like they were too shameful to speak about. Since meeting Ste, I had gone completely full circle, sharing my innermost secrets with the media, with politicians, with everyone. I worried Ste might one day regret his involvement and decide the exposure was all too much. But for now, he seemed to relish the battle.

Whilst he was busy contacting MPs and council leaders, I threw myself into planning our big day, booked for October 25, 2014. I went all out for a traditional white wedding, with 30 guests at Oldham Register Office followed by a party for around 50 in the evening. Our wedding seemed to tie together the skills I enjoyed most: organising and picking out colour schemes!

Granny Pat was, by now, not well enough to leave her house, but she helped me design our wedding invitations, and she paid for my hair and make-up too. I couldn't wait for our big day. The register office was pinned in my memory as a place of trauma. It was, after all, where the two attackers had parked, as they waited outside the police station for me after the assault in the churchyard. I associated the register office with pain. But all of that was about to change, because I was determined our big day should be about me and Ste, and not them. The perpetrators had already stolen too much from me and trespassed on so many occasions throughout my life.

'Enough is enough,' I told myself.

Our wedding day, coming on the anniversary of the attacks, marked a new start for me. On the morning, I was zipped into a traditional white ballgown, with a strapless bodice and ruffles down the front. As I arrived at the register office, I felt like one of the Disney princesses I had idolised as a child. I beamed to see our family and friends gathered together as I walked down the aisle.

'You look beautiful,' Ste smiled.

Any nerves I had fluttered away as he took my hands and repeated his vows.

The day was perfect, and if the hulking shadows of my past followed me around, then I chose not to see them.

After dancing the night away, we drove to York, where we spent a romantic honeymoon in a cosy lodge. As we sipped champagne in our hot tub, I was filled with happiness. And for the first time since I was eight years old, I felt truly loved and safe.

23

PAUL WAITES was listed to stand trial at Manchester's Minshull Street Crown Court the following year. It was the same court where Shakil Chowdhury had been convicted, and also where the online paedophiles we'd snared had appeared. The idea of returning there for yet another trial was daunting. But with Ste by my side, I felt strong.

'Would you like to look around the court?' an officer asked me. 'Familiarise yourself?'

'No thank you,' I replied drily. 'That place is etched on my mind.'

With just a few weeks to go, I was advised Waites was pleading not guilty, as he had maintained all the way through since his arrest.

'Is there anything else at all you can think of?' the officer asked. 'Any single detail that might strengthen your case?'

'No,' I replied. 'I'm sorry. It's so long ago. I think I've blocked a lot of it out.'

The more I tried to visualise those three meetings, the further they seemed to stretch away from me, like a car disappearing into the distance. Accessing an old memory was like snatching at a cloud, and it dissolved as soon as my fingers curled around it. But one evening, a random memory suddenly popped into my head, where I had once called Waites from my mother's landline. My mobile phone had been on the blink and so I had risked using the family phone instead.

'Perhaps there's a record of that?' I suggested.

My old pay-as-you-go mobile phone was long gone and I hadn't kept text messages or call logs. Besides, Waites had always insisted I delete all our communication. I hoped this new information might be useful, but still, I knew it wasn't enough. It didn't prove what he had done to me. The night before the trial, rigid with anxiety, I struggled to sleep. Blurry reminders flashed across the back of my mind: the bandana, the sunglasses, the two hands grabbing either side of my head.

'Come on, baby.'

Suddenly, I sat bolt upright in bed.

'Ste!' I shrieked. 'He has a mole on his groin! Waites has a mole! I can see it in my mind, crystal clear.'

'Sam, that's vital evidence,' he mumbled, still half-asleep but already smiling. 'Well done.'

Early the next morning, I messaged the officer dealing with my case.

'How sure are you?' he asked. 'We need 99% or better.'

'Yes,' I confirmed. 'I'm that sure. I will swear to it.'

We arrived at the court and were shown to the same basement room I'd waited in for Chowdhury's trial. I even remembered the Xbox games and the children's books in a box in the corner. The start time of his trial came and went and still, we waited. My nerves were shredded. But Ste reassured me.

'This is good news. You've produced a golden nugget of evidence for the prosecution. Waites and his defence will have to decide how they react to it. The pressure is on them and not on you.'

Eventually, my barrister popped his head around the door and beckoned me into a different room, where a solicitor and police officer were waiting. I knew, from their broad smiles, that it was good news.

'Waites has changed his plea,' my barrister announced. 'It's over, Samantha. Well done. That last piece of evidence was extremely useful for us.'

In April 2015, Paul Waites was jailed for 11 years for rape, four years concurrently for causing or inciting sexual activity with an underage child, three years concurrently for sexual assault, two years concurrently for sexual assault, and 12 months concurrently for sexual grooming. Waites was also subjected to a Sexual Harm Prevention Order, restricting his use of the internet and association with children. He was described in court as a former teacher, aged 42, who lived in Leeds. In a separate case, he had previously been jailed for six years in 2009 for filming himself sexually abusing young girls and possessing indecent images of children.

Judge Maurice Greene said Waites targeted girls and had also asked me for sexually explicit images. He said:

'You essentially groomed her over a period of months. Hopefully, in time, she will learn to live with what you and others have done to her, but it will never go away.'

Ste had helped me to prepare a statement to the court, and in it, I said:

'Paul Waites has ruined my life. He has permanently damaged me. I was using the internet as a normal 12-year-old girl. I confided in him about my life and problems, and he used that to control me. He became angry or nasty if I wouldn't meet him. He targeted me because of my age and made me feel like he was the only one I could trust. He took away my childhood… I deliberately changed my appearance so I didn't look like me… I felt like a prisoner in my own mind. I grew up afraid of men; I had five years of my life where having a relationship with a man wasn't an option, because of what he had done to me… Because of what Paul Waites did to me I couldn't trust anyone, he took me away from my family and manipulated me so that I came away from them, I hated them. He turned me against them and isolated me from the world… He made me do sexual things on a webcam and then took advantage of me when I met him in his car… He recorded me and made me physically gag like I was going to be sick… Waites made me believe I could trust anything a stranger said. I believe this directly resulted in what happened to me in October 2006. As a result of what Waites did to me, there was a perception I was voluntarily sexually active, which I believe had a significant impact on people's opinion of me and the justice system's leniency with my attackers. I thought I could trust him, and when I was in trouble, I rang Waites for help and he couldn't care less. Paul Waites has ruined my life.'

I felt reassured that Waites was behind bars, satisfied he had received a long sentence and pleased he would be off the streets and away from other children for the next few years at least. But the trial, and the build-up to it, had been draining.

I hadn't slept properly for months. My mind was a jumble of memories and flashbacks, of witness statements and complaints. It seemed to me that we rushed from one meeting to the next, from one court case to the next and it was time to press pause, or even stop.

'I need some time to take all of this in,' I said to Ste. 'I want to take a break from the campaign and focus on my job and on the house. Maybe we could decorate our bedroom?'

Ste frowned.

'Don't you see this is exactly the right time to carry on the campaign?' he replied. 'We need to get predators like Waites off the streets. The police have to protect children. Social services have to listen to children.'

I nodded wearily. I knew he was right. I just didn't feel up to it right at this moment. Yet neither did I feel I could step away from our campaign. Ste had done so much for me. He had dedicated his entire life to pursuing justice for me and for other victims of grooming for the past two years. He had taken on my suffering and my shame as though by osmosis and he had turned it right around. I was so grateful, and I owed him big time. He deserved my full support. And yes, this was how it was starting to feel – that Ste deserved *my* support, with *his* campaign. This was beginning to feel like his fight and not mine. But I ignored the niggling worries of doubt, telling myself not to be so picky. I was lucky to have Ste. I knew that.

'I'll carry on with the campaign,' I agreed. 'You're absolutely right.'

Not long after, I got a letter from the CPS to say they had

lost two laptops that contained sensitive information relating to the Paul Waites case. My interviews, along with interviews by the victims of Jimmy Savile's former chauffeur, Ray Teret, were missing. I was horrified, worrying my interviews might be posted online or on social media by whoever had stolen them. I felt I could not cope with any more exposure. My private life felt like a free-for-all, a lucky dip in which people could pick a parcel and unwrap it to learn more about my personal hurt and humiliation.

'See!' Ste said, waving the letter in the air as though it was ammunition. 'This is what we are dealing with. This is why we have to fight this system. The CPS are a disgrace.'

He was correct. I knew that. But I was so pre-occupied with worrying about my own privacy that I didn't have the headspace to take on the entire system, too. Each time I logged on to Facebook or Instagram, I dreaded seeing my face plastered across the screen.

Samantha Roberts police interview! Hear how she was duped by Paul Waites! Exclusive!

Like a flesh-eating bug, the attacks had eaten away at me from the inside out, all through my teenage years. But now, the campaign seemed to be chipping away at me from the outside in. I felt as though every piece of information I shared publicly was another physical piece of me lost. Soon there would be nothing left of me at all.

Eight days on, the laptop was located, and following an investigation by the Information Commissioner's Office (ICO), the CPS was slapped with a £200k penalty. Ironically, the true victims of the theft received nothing. I was still reeling from the CPS's mistake when I got another letter to say that, due to storage issues at GMP, the evidence in my case had been destroyed. Ste was livid.

'There are guilty men out there, walking around free!' he seethed. 'And now the evidence has gone!'

He was referring to the bedsheets, the towels, the used condoms, the clothing and the personal effects from the car and the two houses. But I thought immediately of my outfit from that day, and the way my belongings had been packed into evidence bags and taken away.

'Grey and white top, pink knickers, white bra, black and pink FCUK jacket, white top, black shorts, blue jeans, bus pass, 84p…'

I'd waited months to get them back, especially my dungarees and my FCUK jacket. At 12, it had seemed to me hideously unjust that I was forced to part with my favourite clothes. Eight years on, they'd been incinerated without officers even offering me the opportunity to collect them. In truth, I would not have wanted them back, they were tainted and contaminated. I did not have the stomach to ever look again at my clothes or at those coins. 84p. What a bargain I had been. Like Ste, I was angry. I was also scared and disappointed. But I recognised these emotions were futile. I couldn't change what had happened. The evidence had gone. When I tried to explain to Ste, he replied:

'Yes, but that's exactly it. We can't change the past, but we can change the future. We need to make sure this doesn't happen again. And who knows, Sam, if you get the justice that you deserve, it might make you feel a whole lot better about your own future.'

As always, I conceded he was right. I needed answers and he was working selflessly to find them for me. Night after night, while I watched TV or I worked on redesigning our home, Ste spent hours scrolling through his laptop, reading reports, making complaints, or researching a particular point of law. He continued to press the police and CPS for information. One day, I came home from work to find him standing, furious, in the middle of the living room.

'You won't believe what I've found out,' he announced. 'The passenger in Chowdhury's car was identified. Chowdhury supplied the name, and the authorities knew who he was. But he was never charged.'

'Are you sure?' I asked. 'Absolutely sure?'

In disbelief, I read the email, which confirmed everything he had said. It was a blow that brought me almost to my knees. Staggering on to a dining chair, I allowed my head to fall into my hands.

'Why?' I asked helplessly. 'Why was he never charged? Why isn't he in prison?'

Those old feelings of worthlessness rushed back in, like fast-flowing water.

I was hit with another bombshell soon after, when, as part of a report, Ste received information that the wife of another one of my alleged attackers had given the police his name in relation to that night. He was not charged and instead he battered her for her disloyalty. Again, it beggared belief. The poor woman had risked her life in order to do the right thing, and nobody was interested. Ste also discovered that one of the suspects in my case lived on the street where I had worked for a year as a mobile carer. My skin crawled as I visualised myself walking down that street every morning, oblivious to the fact that a man who had raped me was behind one of the doors, just a few feet away. It felt to me that the police, the CPS and the courts were sending me a very clear message: they did not care about what I had been through, and they did not care about removing my attackers from the streets. For me, this was a final confirmation, which had been building in layers, year after year, that I did not matter.

'I'm going to do something about this,' Ste promised. 'I won't let them get away with it.'

Numbly, I nodded. Again, I felt pulled in two directions – grateful for his support, but smothered by it also. For me, each piece of news was a body blow that I needed time to recover from. For Ste, each piece of news whetted his appetite to keep on digging and fighting. On his laptop, he had a long list of bulletpoints:

- How did Sam slip through the net of social services? She told them about Paul Waites – why was this not investigated further?
- Sam had attended a sexual health clinic for condoms and a pregnancy test – why was this not investigated further?
- Sam was vulnerable, due to her ADHD and autism – why was she not protected?
- Why did an officer send Sam away when she tried to report the sexual assault in the churchyard?

- Why, on the night of the gang rapes, were no attackers picked up on CCTV or identified by eyewitnesses, despite two of them waiting outside a police station for her?
- Why, despite Sam leading police to the two houses, and forensic testing showing several types of semen, was only Shakil Chowdhury convicted? Why were there no more charges even after two more names were provided?
- Why did police not investigate Sam's reference to Paul Waites in her interview after the rapes?
- Why did Chowdhury only get six years for his heinous crimes? Why did he only serve three years? Why was he not deported? Why was he living in a hostel near a primary school?

Why, why, why?

The questions went on and on and the list, like the torture, was endless.

But as much as I would have liked the answers, I also wanted – and needed – a normal life. We were young newlyweds – this was supposed to be the best time of our lives. Mentally, I knew the attacks had damaged me irreversibly. Those men would sit and squat in my head forever, regardless of how much I campaigned. But practically, we didn't need them in our daily lives. We needed freedom.

'You will not defeat me,' Ste smiled, as he saw me reading his list. 'Remember our slogan?'

I forced a smile back. But inside, I was beginning to suspect that the thing to defeat me might just be the campaign itself.

24

AFTER MONTHS of requests, letters and phone calls, Ste presented me with two huge bundles of notes.

'These are all your police interviews and your social services notes,' he said. 'We can go through them together and see what we find.'

'Wow!' I replied, amazed to see how thick each bundle was.

In truth, I was frightened of reading my own records. I wasn't sure I was strong enough to relive it all. So many of my bad memories were crammed into a cupboard in my mind with the door firmly closed. I didn't want them all spilling out again and making a mess.

'Let's start reading these records tonight,' Ste said.

I didn't know how to say no to him. I didn't know how to refuse. Besides, his enthusiasm was infectious and it would have been cruel of me to dampen it. I reminded myself how lucky I was to have a husband like him. That night, as we sat side by side on the sofa, I prepared myself for more shocks, more heartache, more failures.

The police notes confirmed that forensic testing had found DNA from at least three individuals through semen stains on my underwear and clothing. Tests on the condoms that had been retrieved from the bedroom showed DNA from four or more individuals. It was staggering to me, even then, that they had been unable to press charges on more than one man. The transcripts of my police interviews left me in tears. In one exchange, I said:

'This is partly my fault for drinking.'

And I had asked:

'Am I going to get into trouble for drinking? Will I get told off cos I'm only 12?'

Aged 12, my view of the world, jarring with the nature of the crimes against me, was essentially childish. When the interviewing officer asked if I had tried to resist the passenger kissing me and touching me, I replied:

'I was too scared if he hit me… or stab me or something.'

What stood out from the transcripts was the lack of communication or conversation from any of the attackers. They had not spoken to me, except to order me to undress or to turn over. They took what they wanted and treated me not as a person, but as a piece of meat. In one interview, I said:

'He had sex with me and I said no four times but he just ignored me and carried on.'

I also read the section of my interview where I had admitted to calling Paul Waites.

'If I tell you anything, do you have to tell my mum?' I asked the officers.

'Would you tell my mum?'

Eventually, I admitted to them that, after the churchyard assault, I phoned 'my mate, Paul…Waites.'

I told the police that I was chatting to him on MSN. And I said:

'I've met him before.'

'Will he get in trouble or anything?'

'He's 18.'

'Do I have to mention it?'

I was a vulnerable child, the victim of a horrendous sex attack, and yet the police did not feel it necessary, or even advisable, to investigate Paul Waites further. Instead, they used the exchange against me when, years later, I reported him for raping me. Reading the interview brought it all crashing back and I remembered again how numb and confused I had felt. How I'd been longing for a bath, desperate to wash off the stains and the damage. If only it were that simple.

In the police notes, after I had reported Paul Waites in 2015, an officer asked:

'Why have you decided to do something about this now, despite the other investigation of gang rape being completed.'

It was there again. The finger of blame more than implicitly pointed at me. All my life I had fought against guilt as my default setting, and the police had reinforced it. Automatically, this was all my fault.

My social services notes held more shocks and confirmed that my social worker knew I was having a relationship with a young adult, aged 18 or 19.

In their notes, I was described as 'controlling and difficult', 'rules the roost' and 'attention seeking'.

One social worker wrote:

'Sam is a very strong character and finds it easy to get her own way' and 'she runs rings round everyone'.

My notes read: 'When Sam was seen at home, she talked about having a 16-year-old boyfriend whom she had not met in person yet, but that she talked to over MSN. She stated that she would be worried about meeting him…'

There were more references to:

'Attention-seeking behaviour' and 'behaviour [is] challenging and puzzling'.

'She has started saying recently that she is intending to run away.'

One entry, quite incredibly, recorded on the same day, stated:

'Sam appeared to be in good spirits… Sam said she had drank the bleach.'

On another day, a social worker wrote:

'She was meeting a man from the internet after I had seen her this afternoon. Also Sam's [relative] phoned manager to say she was concerned about Sam meeting an older man. Met Sam and told her that we were all concerned about her meeting this man from the internet, again I stressed why a boy of 18 years would knowingly keep contact with a girl of 12. Sam said I could meet him and show me that he is okay. Again we discussed the dangers.'

After one meeting, I read that the aim of the session had been 'to discuss dangers of internet dating and safety issues'.

I was appalled at the terminology. How could I have been 'dating' aged 12? This was not dating. Just as it was not, as the police had previously claimed, a 'relationship'. This was child sexual abuse. I didn't understand why that was so difficult to grasp. With each page, and each observation, a rising swell of anger vibrated through my body:

'Sam says she has been in contact with a man of 19 from the internet, she says she has met him once in Sainsbury's car park. Again I stressed the dangers to Sam, also that it was illegal to have sex with a young girl.'

'It is very difficult to know when Sam is telling the truth or inventing stories.'

More damaging than my anger was the overwhelming sadness that the person I thought was trying to help me was in fact writing nasty and unfounded criticism about me instead. Reading over my past – an incident where I self-harmed with a kitchen knife, the time when I had drunk bleach from the bathroom – brought it all back again in full, frightening technicolour. Each scene played out across my eyeline: horrific visuals that turned my stomach to acid. The bile was sour in my throat. In one meeting, I had said to my social worker that I was: 'eight out of ten unhappy' and I wanted to go into care. In response, they wrote that 'Samantha talked about sleeping on the street or wanting to go into a children's home' and that I had an 'idealised view of being in care'.

Their words seemed absolutely heartless and without compassion, understanding or care. I had worried, all through those years, that none of the adults around me liked me. And it seemed I was right.

25

I WAS still reeling from the contents of my social services notes when my beloved Granny Pat passed away. She had been battling heart problems and a serious infection. Right up to her death. She and I had spent most Friday nights together, playing cards and eating bowls of cereal, just like the old days. I had loved her dearly, she had been the one constant through my childhood, my shining light in the dark, and her death hit me hard.

'Thank you, Granny Pat,' I whispered as I ordered her funeral flowers, which spelled simply: 'Granny'.

That same week, my period was late and I at first blamed it on the stress of losing my grandmother. But by the weekend, I decided to do a pregnancy test. When it was positive, Ste and I were overjoyed.

'I can't wait to be a dad,' he beamed. 'We can be a proper family. I'm so pleased, Sam.'

'Me too,' I grinned.

I wished Granny Pat could have shared my news, but at the same time I felt the pregnancy could be a final gift from her and a way of making me smile through my grief. It was a comfort to know she was looking down on me still.

A scan showed we were having a little boy, and as the months passed, the physical aspect of my pregnancy went well. But I had a small gremlin, gnawing at my brain, whose voice became louder and more raucous as my bump grew. I could not help thinking back to the messages I'd received, at the start of our campaign, from other survivors of grooming gangs.

Some had been through the courts and had received justice of sorts. Others had not been able to make a report to police. Some had been in care. Most had troubled family backgrounds and poor bonds with their mothers. And all, with no exception, had struggled to be mothers themselves.

Most of the women I had spoken to had been unable to raise their own children. It was a depressing cycle and now, as I reached my due date, I became fixated by the worry that I would be swallowed up by it too. I suffered with surges of anxiety, which at times were so fierce they almost pinned me to my bed.

'You'll never be able to bring up a child, Sam,' said the gremlin in my head. 'You're damaged. You're broken.'

The worst thing was, I believed it. I felt I was doomed as a mother. After a long and difficult labour at St Mary's Hospital, Manchester, I gave birth by caesarean section to a beautiful little boy named Joshua. Cradling him in my arms, I was awash with love.

'Hello darling,' I whispered, kissing his tiny nose. 'I'm your mummy. Welcome to the world.'

But even then, with my baby in my arms and Ste by my bedside, I had a frightening premonition that this happiness would not, could not, last. After Joshua was born, I gave up work to be a full-time mum. Ste, having completed his law degree, was now working in cyber security and studying for a master's degree. He was extremely busy, yet still, like a sponge, he absorbed every small detail connected to my case. Night after night, he tapped away on his laptop, firing off complaints to Greater Manchester Police, Oldham Council and our MP.

'Sign this, Sam,' he'd say, pushing a pen and paper under my nose. 'I need your consent to act on your behalf.'

Wordlessly, I signed, before turning back to Joshua in his baby rocker. Our son was only a few weeks old when, in bed one night, I felt Ste's hands moving under my pyjamas.

'No,' I said sleepily. 'I'm not ready yet, Ste.'

I was still sore from the caesarean and exhausted by the birth. But Ste didn't stop.

'No,' I said again, louder this time.

But it was as though he couldn't hear me. As though I was 12 years old and trapped in Shakil Chowdhury's house and nobody was interested in what I thought. Afterwards, in floods of tears, I said:

'You knew I didn't want that. You didn't listen.'

Ste had been encouraging me to find my voice for so long. And now, when I needed it most, he had silenced me. I did not even get to make decisions about my own body.

'If you really feel that I did something wrong, you should go to the police,' Ste said.

I knew these were the tactics he used, his best form of defence was always attack. Yet still, I felt wrong-footed and confused. I had been very clear that I didn't want sex. But I didn't want to break up our little family. And this was not the same, I told myself, as the rapes when I was a child. I associated rape with deep trauma, and I had become desensitised to the point that I could explain Ste's behaviour away.

My ADHD, so often a problem in my childhood, was useful as an adult to help me move on quickly from distress. I did not speak to the police, but instead confided in Ste's mum, Maria, who promised to support me whatever I decided. The following month, I missed a period and discovered I was pregnant again.

This was an unexpected twist. But again, I kidded myself that the whole thing had perhaps been a misunderstanding, a moment of madness, or extreme weakness, from Ste. With another baby on the way, I had to move on from it. I felt I had no other choice. Ste did not mention the incident again, so I did not mention it either. As always, I followed his lead.

The months flew by and soon I was back in hospital, enjoying my first cuddle with our second child, a daughter named Maya. Looking after two babies was hectic and I hardly had a moment to myself. Like most new mums, I longed to take a shower in peace or have a spare five minutes to do my make-up. Like Joshua, Maya had been a caesarean delivery, so I needed longer to recover.

I had presumed, without us even discussing it, that the campaign would be shifted on to the back burner, now that we had two children to think of. But Ste didn't see it that way at all. If anything, he seemed to spend more time on his laptop. He devoted every evening to emailing an MP or calling a council leader. He was forever putting in requests for files and records relating to my case. Like all parents of young children, we were short of time, sleep and money, and we bickered.

'Ste, we have a family. I need some help please,' I said. 'I can't do this on my own, and I don't want to. I don't need a campaigner. I need a husband and a father for our kids.'

'Sure,' he replied, absent-mindedly without even looking up from his screen.

My caesarean scar was still tender, but he didn't seem to notice me wincing in pain when I picked Joshua up. Instead, he said:

'Look at this reply from the forensic team. I'm going to complain.'

Some evenings, I'd hand Maya to him whilst I went to bath Joshua. But he simply slotted her under his arm while he continued typing, oblivious to her sweet little gurgles. It saddened me that he wasn't enjoying fatherhood the way I'd hoped. I'd hardly given the campaign a second thought since our children were born, but it seemed to be all that Ste thought about. I felt like a passenger on his runaway train and endless quest for justice. He was veering dangerously out of control.

'Stop this train! I want to get off!' I wanted to say.

But instead, I watched sadly as he organised files and made notes, so busy that he missed Maya's first smile and Joshua's first steps. After Maya turned one, I found I out I was expecting another baby. The bigger part of me was thrilled, I loved being a mother, and every new life was a blessing. But I also worried how I'd cope. Most days, I felt like a single parent.

'We'll manage,' Ste promised, kissing the top of my head.

But for the first time ever, I was starting to really doubt him. My third pregnancy seemed to pass him by completely. As he was consumed with campaigning, I was equally focused on our children and our home. For the first time, I was also starting to feel lonely in my marriage, and the Ste-shaped scaffolding that had held me up for so long was now cracking and collapsing around me. It felt like we were on different sides. I realised it was possible to spend time with someone and yet also miss the person who they used to be.

Lonely and afraid, old habits from the past caught up with me and I began comfort-eating, stuffing the void between us with crisps, chocolate and snacks. I'd carried weight since I was a child and had always been grateful that Ste never commented or pushed me to diet. But now, hitting a dress size 24, it really was getting me down. As my pregnancy bump grew bigger, I became mentally and physically exhausted. And the words of my attacker, branded on the back of my eyelids, returned to haunt me:

'You have a big belly.'

I felt myself sliding and I struggled to cope. I knew now, how marathon runners felt when they hit a wall. I could hardly put one foot in front of the other, and that was nothing to do with my weight. Each day was a challenge. Yet Ste did not even seem to notice. In November 2019, we were notified that Oldham Council would be carrying out a child sexual exploitation (CSE) review, partially in response to our campaign. Ste was over the moon. But I was so engrossed with looking after our children and our unborn child that I barely gave it much thought.

'I need you to sign this form, give permission for these files to be released,' said Ste.

He didn't even check what I thought first. Miserably, I did as he said. But afterwards, I had a sudden jolt of realisation. I didn't want to see any more files. I didn't want any more bad news. I had enough to cope with for the moment. Sorting through the permanent pile of paperwork on our dining table, I found the relevant forms and rang the number on the top.

'I'm sorry for the mix-up, but I'm withdrawing my permission,' I said. 'I don't feel up to it.'

Something stopped me from telling Ste what I'd done. I suspected he might be angry, or at the very least, frustrated. I didn't want to appear ungrateful. A couple of evenings later, I went up to bed, leaving him working, as usual, on his laptop. Sometime afterwards, I stirred a little as he came into the bedroom. And then, I felt a sharp pain on the back of my heel, as though I'd been stung.

'Ow!' I yelled, flinging back the duvet.

I expected to see a winter wasp or a bee on the sheet. To my confusion, there was a small nick on my heel, bleeding slightly. And Ste was standing at the end of the bed, holding a penknife.

'Why did you withdraw your permission?' he asked, his voice shaking with anger. 'I am trying to help you, Sam.'

I was stunned, and more than a little scared. I had been

through so much worse in my life and yet this small aggression, from the man I loved, shook me to my core. Ste was my saviour and my soulmate. Why had he turned on me?

'I'm sorry,' I mumbled, pressing a tissue on my heel. 'I just can't manage anything else at the moment.'

Ste just couldn't see it. We barely spoke for a few days, and when we did, it was for him to push yet another form under my nose.

'Can you sign this?' he asked.

'No,' I replied. 'I'm not doing it. I can't.'

I saw the glint of his penknife as he pulled it from his pocket and he pressed the tip, just for a moment, into my hand. Bewildered, I staggered backwards, pulling down my sleeve to stop the bleeding.

'What's wrong with you?' I asked. 'Why are you treating me like this? I've told you I don't want to carry on with the campaign. I want to focus on the kids. I'm about to give birth, Ste, and I need your support.'

But the more I reached out, the further he seemed to turn in on himself. He was so fixed on the campaign that there was no room for anyone else in his life, not even his wife and his children. It broke my heart that the thing that had pulled us so close together was now driving us apart. I'd fallen for Ste partly because he had made me feel safe, but now I was afraid of who he was becoming.

Not long after, I gave birth to a second daughter, Danielle, by caesarean section. Parallel to my joy and excitement was the acceptance that my marriage was sadly and inevitably coming to an end. Back at home, my recovery from surgery was slow. Scans showed I had a blood clot, and I needed a further operation to have it removed. The op went well, but afterwards I needed Ste's support more than ever. Instead, his behaviour became more and more peculiar. He had always kept records of our spending. Like me, he was organised and meticulous. It had seemed a good idea at the start, to ensure we didn't spend more than we earned, and I was all in favour of his checks and his lists. But after Danielle was born, his prudence mutated into an ugly obsession. One day, I came home from the supermarket, and he presented me with a spreadsheet, labelled: 'Asda'.

'Please list every item you've bought, along with the price,' he said, in a way that made me feel I could not refuse.

He waited quietly whilst I checked each product off my receipt and he then cross-checked each figure with the website prices, to make sure I was telling the truth.

'Ste, this is ridiculous,' I protested.

But it became a pattern every time I went to the shops. I was forced to declare everything: nappies, washing-up liquid, even a 20p ride for the girls outside the supermarket. Like the campaign, this had started out with the best intentions, but along the way it had become warped, controlling and wrong. I realised the problem was not the campaign itself, rather it was Ste's controlling approach.

'You should see a doctor,' I suggested. 'I think you might be depressed.'

But Ste would not hear of it. He thought he could manage his own mental health problems. Typically, he did not like accepting help or advice from anyone. It was an attribute that had made him so strong and formidable, but it was also his weakness. More than once, I made him an appointment with the GP, but he refused to go. Meanwhile, his control grew tighter and tighter until I began to feel like I had a pair of hands around my neck. More than anyone, I knew emotional turmoil was tough and I wanted to support him. But no amount of mental illness gave him the right to abuse me. I felt trapped and I didn't know what to do.

Ste flew into a rage one day because I'd bought milk at the corner shop and forgotten to declare it on his spreadsheet. I just couldn't understand this compulsion. I didn't overspend or secretly spend. I didn't buy myself luxuries or gifts. Ste had no reason to doubt me or to worry about my budgeting.

'Why are you doing this?' I asked. 'What's happened to you?'

He was sitting right next to me and yet he could have been on another planet. I thought of the young man who had cooked me a curry and held my hand while I cried about my past. Where had he gone? All through my teenage years I had accepted I would never find love. I had judged myself more harshly than any internet troll ever could: a slut, a slag, damaged goods.

I believed I was somehow irreversibly damaged and dirty and that nobody would ever want me. But meeting Ste had blown that miserable theory to pieces. He had shown me love and happiness on a level I would never have thought possible, and he had taught me how to love myself. We had been on such a wonderful journey together. But did that mean I should settle for whatever he did and accept however he behaved towards me? Yes, I was grateful. Yes, I appreci-ated everything he had done for me. But I also resented him deeply. He had vowed to give me a voice in my fight against the men who had attacked me and he had kept his promise. But now, admittedly on a much lower level, Ste was abusing me too.

By forcing me to take part in the campaign, by nicking me with his penknife, by controlling my spending and my lifestyle – he was abusing me. This was not comparable with the childhood grooming, the sexual assaults and the rapes. But it was still abuse. Ste was perpetrating the very problem he was campaigning to eradicate.

As my appointee, he advocated for me, he represented me, he made my decisions. He not only spoke for me, but he spoke over me too. Ironically, I no longer had a voice.

Ste had saved me, but now he was systematically destroy-ing me. My life was spinning out of control, and I was falling fast. And I no longer knew whether I had jumped, or whether Ste had pushed me.

26

ONE MORNING, I arrived home from the school run to find a string of messages on my phone. One, from a reporter on a local newspaper, asked:

'Have you time for a chat about Steven's letter, which we're running today?'

'What letter?' I replied, my heart already sinking.

'The open letter to the leader of the council?' he wrote. 'About the sexual attacks you suffered as a child and how the authorities involved let you down?'

Scrolling frantically through my phone as I searched for the article, I tried to regulate my breathing. But I could feel the anxiety radiating from me. I couldn't believe Ste had done this without my consent, or without even letting me know. Fury pulsed through me as I clicked on the website. But, as I started to read, my anger quickly gave way to sickly fear. Ste's letter to the council spoke of the profound sexual exploitation I had suffered as a child and went on to call out Oldham Council and Greater Manchester Police for failing to protect me. He had listed the attacks, both by Paul Waites and then by the nine men on the night of the gang rapes. It went on to describe how the residents on the street where I was raped had repeatedly told the council about a large-scale grooming operation in which taxis would gather on the street every week and children would be taken to the address in a conveyor belt fashion. The letter was openly critical of the council, and it sought acknowledgement from the council leader and the chief executive to admit that there had been a cover-up of these failings and asked for an apology.

'Oh Ste,' I groaned. 'What have you done?'

He just could not help himself. He had to keep picking fights with the authorities. And if it had been his case, that would have been fine. But it was not. It was mine. And once again, my life was splattered all across the media like spilled milk – the same milk I was forced to record on a spreadsheet every time I bought it.

By the time I'd finished reading, I was slumped on the kitchen floor, sobbing. Reading the article was like ripping off the scabs all over again and watching them bleed. And I wasn't sure they'd ever heal again. When I'd had a cup of tea, I called Ste at work.

'You had no right to do this without my permission,' I told him. 'You've plastered my life all over the local newspaper again! I told you I didn't want any more of this. Did you not think to even check with me first?

'This is the final straw. I can't be a mother to three young children whilst this is happening. I just can't do it.'

Ste was unrepentant. If anything, he seemed put out that I wasn't grateful.

'You need to fill in today's spreadsheet with your Asda

shop,' he reminded me. 'Leave everything to do with the campaign to me. Don't worry about that.'

He just didn't understand! And no matter what he said, I *did* worry. I worried that Ste's campaign would be the end of us because, forced to choose between his family or his fight, he had shown which way he would go.

The following day, we both had something far more serious to concern us when social services, as a result of the open letter, made contact with us. I had a deepening mistrust of social workers from my childhood, made worse since I'd read my notes and seen the unkind things they had written about me.

I was perturbed at the thought of them steamrolling their way into my life once again. But I knew, if Ste continued to antagonise the authorities by splashing my private life all over the media, they had to investigate.

'Early intervention means we can offer you early support,' the social worker explained when she visited.

'That sounds like a good idea,' I said hesitantly.

And when she asked about the children and how we were coping, like a dam bursting, it all spilled out. My fears for our fractured marriage, Ste's control, his violence, and his obsession with the campaign.

'I just don't know what to do,' I said, but even as I spoke, I admitted that wasn't true. I had known, in my heart, for many months.

'I think we should separate,' I told Ste sadly. 'I have to put our children first.'

'No,' he pleaded. 'Don't leave. We can work it out. I'll kill myself if you go.'

His words were like a prison door clanging behind me. By making me responsible for his safety and for his life, he was effectively laying a trap for me. I reminded myself Ste had once pulled me out of a very dark place and that I should do the same for him now. But the difference was, he didn't want my help. He just wanted me to do as he said. I had tried to get him to see a doctor, or to seek counselling, and he could not admit he had a problem. Meanwhile he was controlling everything I did – and he was abusive. Our marriage was no longer healthy for me or our children, nor for him.

'Ste, we can't carry on like this,' I told him. 'I'm sorry.'

With a heavy heart, I began making plans for life without him. I applied to get my old job as a carer back, knowing I would need to start earning my own wage. With the children in school and nursery, I could at least work part-time and support myself. And that way I would not be forced to declare every penny I spent on Ste's awful spreadsheets. And I knew Ste would contribute too. He loved his family. I was sure, deep down, he was still a decent man. He just couldn't show it anymore. I had a sliver of worry that, with his legal expertise, our divorce might become messy in court. But it was a chance I had to take.

And then, with the worst possible timing, I missed a period. When a pregnancy test confirmed I was pregnant, I shook my head in gloomy denial. Whilst Ste was at work, I bought another test, just to be sure, and was careful to pay in cash. Then I buried both in the outside bin.

'What am I going to do?' I sobbed, curled up on the end of my bed.

The prospect of raising another child on my own was too daunting. I had my hands more than full with our three young children. Ste came home from work, opened his laptop, and began typing. I hovered by the doorway, my secret heavy in my chest, but I couldn't find the right words to tell him. I suspected he would use the pregnancy as yet more ammunition to make me stay with him. It was going to be difficult to leave him as it was, without the added complication of a new baby. When the kids were in bed, I went up myself too.

'Goodnight,' I said to Ste, but he was so busy typing, I wasn't sure he heard me.

Awake all night, I felt desolate and so alone. Before Ste, I'd become accustomed to loneliness. I'd almost used it as a shield against the rest of the world. I had worn it like a badge. But now, having known such happiness and inclusion, this new isolation was harder than ever to cope with.

Two weeks passed and, as I fretted over our future, a low, nagging pain in my stomach barely registered at first. But in the bathroom, I discovered I was bleeding. Holding back my tears, I left the children with a friend and went to the Royal Oldham Hospital. This place held such happy memories for me. I'd loved working here, in the office and the drugs department, and they were the exciting early days of my relationship with Ste too. But today I knew with a heavy heart that my visit would break me in two.

In A&E, doctors confirmed I had suffered a miscarriage, and after checks, I was allowed to go home. Racked with guilt and grief, I drove instead to a quiet spot on the moors. Irrationally, I blamed myself for the miscarriage. I had not wanted another baby and now I had lost it. Had the baby known how I felt? Had my body somehow picked up on my reluctance to go through a fourth pregnancy?

I wept for the baby I would never hold and for the child I would never know. I knew I had to tell Ste about the miscarriage. He had a right to know. I wondered if it might even be a wake-up call for him – a brutal realisation that he needed to concentrate on his family's happiness and not on spreadsheets, or meetings, or complaints. But as I was preparing to drive home, his car suddenly pulled up alongside mine. I could only stare in shock as he tapped on my window.

'Why were you at the hospital?' he demanded. 'And why have you been parked out here for so long? What's going on? Are you having an affair?'

'What?' I gulped. 'No, of course not.'

The cogs of my mind whirred quickly as I worked out he was tracking me in some way. That was the only explanation. I hadn't told anyone I was going to the hospital, or to the moors. Wearily, I accepted I had been foolish to think there might be some way back for us.

'I'm moving out,' I told him. 'I'm sorry, I can't take this anymore.'

By now, into 2020, the first Covid lockdown had started, and so we were not allowed to go and stay with family or friends. Instead, we ended up in a hostel, cramped, cold and dirty. There were bed bugs, and the place stank of stale cigarette smoke, even though there were 'No smoking' signs all over the walls.

As I plonked my case on the floor, I questioned whether I

was doing the right thing. Deep down, I knew Ste's behaviour was unacceptable. But I was still clinging on to every last possibility, every faint hope, that he might undergo a last-minute transformation. Instead, his behaviour just got worse. He bombarded me with calls and messages and sent quotes from our favourite films, all designed to blackmail me emotionally into returning home. With reference to *Forrest Gump*, he wrote:

'Dear God, make me a bird so I can fly far, far, away… Jenny tried to fly away many times… Forrest loved her anyway.'

Another day, he wrote:

'Sometimes the kindest thing you can do for someone is to let them go.'

He sent songs too: *Ain't No Sunshine*, by Bill Withers, *Where's My Love*, by SYML and OneRepublic's *Come Home*.

He sent photos of the children, right from the day they were born. I knew he was trying to make me feel guilty so I would go back to him. And it worked. All I had ever wanted was a normal family and a small slice of happiness. Could I really walk away from everything Ste had given me?

'Come home,' he pleaded. 'You need me, you know you do.'

I felt myself cracking. He was right. He was always right. After all, who had I been when we had first met? How would my life have turned out without him?

My past leaned heavily on me as I remembered the dark days when I had been too afraid to leave my bedroom, and I had slashed at my arms and swallowed bleach to escape the demons in my head. Ste had been the first person, the only person, to actually listen to my story. Not only that, but he had, without hesitation, embraced my suffering as his own and he had fought tirelessly on my behalf. He had ensured Waites was punished. He had exposed the failings of the authorities. Slowly, he was changing the system. And he was doing it all for me.

'I can't carry on without you,' he wrote. 'Please, Sam. One more chance. Think of the kids.'

'Okay,' I agreed, in a moment of weakness. 'I'll come back. But just for a trial period.'

Before I even pressed send, I knew I'd made a mistake. Packing my bags, I was filled with regret, and walking in through the front door just made it worse. Ste had a pile of papers waiting for me to sign. He wanted to discuss the new inquiry that Oldham Council was holding.

'Ste!' I gulped. 'There's no food in the fridge. I need to go to Asda. All this other stuff can wait.'

'It can't,' he replied, pushing a pen into my hand.

He seemed agitated and annoyed, as though he was already no longer happy to have me home.

He wanted my signature, not me.

When I got back with the shopping, he was waiting with his spreadsheet to record my spending.

'Let me see the receipt,' he demanded.

With sadness, I realised nothing had changed and nothing ever would change. At the end of the week, I moved out again. This time, late in March 2020, I was determined to be strong and not to go back. Damaged by the abuse of the past, destroyed by the control of the present, our relationship was over.

Unpacking in another unwelcoming hostel, I felt at rock bottom. Despite everything, I still loved the man Ste had once been. And that was what made it so hard.

27

STE AND I needed to be in contact, for the sake of our children and our divorce. Our house was council-owned but we had been talking about buying a new place away from Oldham and away from all the reminders. We'd even viewed a couple of properties in Keighley, West Yorkshire. But now, that would never happen and we had to plan for two separate homes and work out our finances fairly. There was bad feeling and bitterness from us both and as with the end of any marriage, relations were strained.

Ste continued to send messages and pictures that were designed to pull at my heartstrings. But I told myself I had to toughen up and ignore them. I was worried about him, but I reminded myself I could not be responsible for him. Without doubt, I knew it was the right decision for us to separate and I had to see it through.

In April 2020, just a couple of weeks after our separation, my phone buzzed with a message from Maria, Ste's mum, who had not been able to contact him and was becoming concerned.

'Have you heard from him?' she asked. 'I'm worried. He sent me some odd messages.'

'No,' I replied. 'I've not spoken to him since yesterday. Maybe we should check on him.'

We arranged to meet at our family home, where Ste's car was parked outside. The door was deadlocked from the inside, so my keys were useless. Maria's partner came too, and he climbed the fence and smashed a small window around the back, to let me in through the hallway.

'Ste?' I called. 'Are you home? Are you okay?'

I couldn't help worrying how annoyed he'd be that we'd broken a window, if he was simply out shopping, or maybe he was inside on a Zoom call for work. But upstairs, on the landing, I stopped suddenly. Around our bedroom door I spotted one of Ste's arms dangling off the end of the bed. Rushing in, I found him lying unconscious on top of the duvet. There was a half empty bottle of Jack Daniel's on the bedside table and empty blister packs of pills on the floor.

'Ste!' I screamed.

Frantically, I rang for an ambulance. Together, we dragged him off the bed, slapping his cheeks and shouting his name. By the time paramedics arrived, Ste was already waking up and sheepishly avoiding eye contact.

'I'm sorry,' he muttered. 'I don't know what came over me. I won't do it again.'

'You must promise me never to harm yourself,' I insisted. 'We all love you and need you, Ste. You know that.'

'I promise,' he agreed. 'I will never hurt myself again.'

The paramedics took him to hospital to be checked over and I followed in my car. Physically, he seemed to be fine, but he was referred for mental health support, which he was not keen to accept.

'There's nothing wrong with me. It was a mistake,' he insisted.

When I was sure he was going to be okay, I left him in hospital. I believed his assurances. Ste did not seem like the sort of man to leave a mess behind. Rather, he had walked into a mess when he started the campaign and he had grasped it with both hands. He was a man who found solutions, not a man who caused problems. He was discharged from hospital the following day and I sent a friendly message to ask how he was. But Ste interpreted my concern as a sign we might get back together.

'No,' I told him. 'It's over. It will never change.'

Quickly, our relationship became strained and hostile again. And from his erratic messages, Ste did not seem himself at all. One minute he was upbeat, looking to the future. The next, he was filled with anguish and despair. Early in the morning on May 1, I received a previously scheduled email from Ste, which read: 'You will get an email in one hour. Read it carefully.'

I sighed, presuming it was in connection with dividing up our money, or in relation to his contact with our son and daughters. We didn't seem to be able to exchange a single piece of information without an argument, and this over-for-mality was very typical of Ste – he had always been official and professional. I remembered those first few months of our relationship, the marriage proposal in the cold sea, those delicious curry nights, our trips to and from Westminster.

We had been a unit. A family. How had it come to this? With the girls in school and nursery, I kept myself busy with tasks until, an hour later, Ste's next message arrived. As I clicked on the top line, my blood froze in my veins.

'This is my goodbye…'

Without reading any more, I grabbed my keys and ran from the hostel in my slippers. Once in the car, I called 999, asking police to meet me at the house. I rang Maria too.

'I think he's killed himself!' I gasped. 'Please hurry.'

Gripped by an icy dread, I drove as fast as I dared. It was only a 10-minute journey, but every traffic light was on red, every junction clogged with cars. The roads seemed to conspire against me and my short journey felt like a lifetime. Unhelpfully, I was bombarded with memories of the night I was raped when each attack had seemed to last longer than the entire night. Today, as then, time was twisted and distorted.

By the time I arrived outside our former family home, I was hysterical with panic. I was expecting the door to be deadlocked again, but my key turned easily, and the front door swung open. In that moment, an intense cold trickled upwards from the tips of my toes right to the ends of my long dark hair.

Shivering, I stepped inside. It was eerily silent, and instinctively I kept my eyes down, frightened to look around me. I knew this was a moment in which my life would change forever. I knew that after I looked up, there was no going back. I wanted to hold on to life before this moment for as long as I could. Every cell in my body screamed out against me raising my head. But I had no choice.

'Ste?' I said, in a small voice.

A thick, choking silence was my only reply. With my heart pounding in my chest, I lifted my head and directly in front of me, I saw him hanging at the top of the stairs.

From standing still, time now raced ahead of me. My mind stayed in that same spot, paralysed with shock. But my body ran up the stairs, desperately trying to lift him down.

When I realised I could not manage it, I ran down to the kitchen to grab a knife before hurtling back up the stairs to cut the belt that was attached inside the loft hatch. It took a superhuman strength to half-lift him down, but somehow I managed it. I knew, from the colour of his skin, that it was too late. But in desperation, I began CPR. Maria arrived and we took it in turns to try to save him. I wished the police would hurry. Where were they?

'Wake up,' I begged, my tears soaking his face. 'Don't leave us. Please don't leave us.'

The police eventually came, and I was ushered downstairs by an officer. I knew Ste was gone. Aged just 30, his life was so tragically over. The rest of the day passed in an odd blur, with Ste's family and friends coming to the house, under Covid regulations, to pay their last respects. A friend collected the children for me and I met them for a hug at the top of the street, before she took them back to her house. I knew then they could never return to their home. I would never be able to go in there again without seeing Ste hanging at the top of the stairs.

'Mummy loves you,' I told them. 'But Daddy was poorly, and he had to go to the angels.'

In the days that followed, we were scattered around relatives and friends. I was almost catatonic, unable to care either for myself or my children. Bent double by shock and anger, I could not even do the most basic of tasks. The police told me Ste had killed himself using a length of belt tied inside the loft.

Trust Ste, I thought sadly, to research his own suicide so comprehensively, as he did everything else. The police also revealed that he had completed his first Zoom meeting for work, that morning, before he died. Again, it was so typical of him to maintain his work ethic right to the end. The officers asked me for a copy of Ste's final message, so I had to force myself to read it too. With trembling hands, I clicked on the email.

'To the most special woman in my life, If you're reading this email it means that I'm no longer with you x That doesn't mean that I don't love you or that this is your fault, it means that the pain of living in despair is greater than the pain of death. You are and continue to be the most special person I've ever laid eyes on. You brought me so many happy memories and experiences, you are the most beautiful and wonderful woman I ever met. You deserve to be happy and to continue living a good life with the children, you have to get better Sam, you need to get out of Oldham and move on from the past here.

'We were so close to leaving, I'm sorry I never got you out of here. I'm sorry for many things, I was never good enough. Make sure Joshua, Maya and Danielle know that I love them unconditionally and that just because you're everything to me, doesn't make them nothing. I love each of them without end and I didn't leave them because I don't love them, it's because the only way you can all move on is if I'm not here anymore...

'I died knowing that you love me, that (the children) love their daddy,

and that comforted me in my last moments here in this world. But because of your PTSD you also hate me... I've become the incarnation of all of your anger and hate because of everything that has happened to you. For that, I failed as your husband and deserve to pay the ultimate toll. As long as I am alive you will never recover, so I have traded my life for yours.

'Before all of this happened, we had so many loving memories, we had an unimpeachable love for each other that is reflected in every aspect of our lives — our kids, our house, the changes we've made to this world for the better. I want you to hold on to those memories and move on, I don't want you to remember how I died, I want you to remember the day I put the ring on your finger — our happiest moments.

'Make sure you do right by (the children), don't let them stray and become like us Sam, make sure they have a good life. Please give them my 'Tao Te Ching' book (tell them you pronounce it dao de ching, it means 'the great way of all things') so that they can read it and know who I was, what I believed in and what I was like.

'You can access everything of mine by logging into Google, put in the password... when you login it will ask you to authorise it on my phone — my phone password is your date of birth, like it always has been. My laptop pin is... That will let you access everything of mine in case you need to take care of affairs. Today I authorised... a payment to you upon my death... Buy a house Sam, move on and live a happy life away from here. You can't live in that prison forever. Let my death mean something, let it be the thing you needed to come back to us. The last thing I want to leave you with is this:

https://www.youtube.com/watch?v=5YXVMCHG-Nk

Remember me, my beautiful wife. I died remembering our special moment.

Yours, Steven

I had plumbed the depths of sadness and heartbreak in my life, but nothing could have prepared me for this. Sobbing, I clicked on the link, which led to our wedding song: *The Blower's Daughter.* I felt so angry at him and yet so sorry for him, too. Had there really been no other way? I read again his claim.

As long as I am alive you will never recover, so I have traded my life for yours.

I didn't understand whether he was trying to urge me to live my life and to continue in a world where he could not. Or was it that he resented my trauma, dragging him down and eventually driving him to suicide? In kinder moments, I could see that Ste had become so fixated on the campaign that it had consumed him and swallowed him alive.

When it finally spat him back out, he had lost the will to carry on. Unlike the story of Jonah and the whale, there could be no happy ending for him. But on other days, I raged at him for executing what I saw as my ultimate punishment for leaving him. Though he insisted he did not blame me, his email was littered with phrases that I felt were designed to make me feel bad and my role in his death was, for him, more than a mere implication.

I've become the incarnation of all of your anger and hate because of everything that has happened to you…

That doesn't mean that I don't love you or that this is your fault…

the only way you can all move on is if I'm not here anymore…

Blighted by guilt and anger, I read and re-read his message. He had saddled our children with a life-long scar and at my lowest points I felt his behaviour was unforgiveable and inexcusable. I did not care what he did to me or how he blamed me. But the damage to our children was irreparable. By pressing the self-destruct button in his own life, he had blown the rest of us to smithereens too.

'Why?' I asked, over and over. 'Why?'

28

OUR TWO younger children did not attend Ste's funeral at Hollinwood Crematorium, Oldham. They were still too young to understand that he had died and I wanted to protect them from the inevitable outpourings of grief and pain. But Joshua insisted he wanted to be there. And in the darkness of the day, he and I shared moments of pure joy.

At the service, I played Johnny Cash's *Ring of Fire*, which Ste had loved to sing. It was a macabre choice and exactly suited his sense of humour. Despite everything, I wanted to give him a good send-off. For so long, he had been a brilliant man, shining so brightly that eventually he had crashed and burned.

The funeral brought no comfort and closure, and afterwards, I struggled to cope with my pain. I was not sleeping or eating, and in a matter of months, I lost 7st, dropping from 20st down to 13. Normally, I would have been thrilled by such effortless weight loss. But I barely noticed as my clothes hung off me and my face thinned. I felt like a faded photograph of my former self, a hollowed-out shell, without substance or structure. Again, as after the attacks, I was losing my sense of self.

Months on, the children and I were still moving around friends and family. I relied on a close friend, Debbie, who took us under her wing like a mother hen. We had not returned to our family home and by the time I felt able to empty it and go through Ste's possessions, they had already been divided amongst people who had claimed to be close to him. It was a cruel blow and further confirmation of how alone I was. I needed Ste to help me out of my grief, yet he was the one who had caused it.

We received his ashes and I scattered some at the cemetery, some in North Wales where he had proposed and some in Minehead, where he had been on holiday as a child. The rest went into storage for our three children. Meanwhile, they had no stability or routine and they needed to go back to nursery and to school. They needed to feel safe and happy and I could not give them that. Not on my own.

I felt I was no longer the best person to care for them. After losing Ste, I had been plunged into grief, guilt, and anguish. But none of this came close to the emotions that ripped through me as, with my heart broken, I came to this realisation.

Memories flickered in my mind of the days of their births and how I had feared, deep down, that the lasting legacy of the grooming, the final and most cruel twist of the blade, would be that I was not able to raise my children. With my prophecy realised, I accepted with a numb finality that girls like me, damaged, abused and broken, did not get to keep their babies. We did not get a happy ending. We did not deserve it.

For days and weeks, with my head in my hands, I wept. I spent hours staring at the tattoo on my arm; how I hated it now.

You have not defeated me

Tasteless and untrue, the words seemed to mock me now. The whole concept was a lie. Ste was well and truly defeated. I was all but broken. Our campaign was in tatters. My second tattoo, our wedding date, had been intended to distract me from the anniversary of the rapes, to replace that dreadful day with a happy one. Instead, it now symbolised double the pain, double the suffering, and double the loss.

'Why, Ste?' I asked again. 'Why did you leave us like this?'

An inquest into his death was held in April 2021 at Rochdale Coroner's Court. Family members complained there had been a lack of mental health support for Ste, but the coroner ruled an 'appropriate' assessment was conducted by Pennine Care's mental health team. I found it difficult, in my evidence, to brush over those uncomfortable truths I did not want recorded or reported. For our children's sake, I wanted him to be remembered as the man he had once been and not the man he was before his death.

There was criticism at the hearing of Greater Manchester Police, who had graded my call for help as a 'two' on the priority scale, something which I argued could have had an impact on the chances of saving Ste.

A report conducted by GMP concluded that the call should have been graded as a 'one' priority and that the call handler 'lacked empathy' and even at certain points sounded 'impatient' with me when I called. It was a tragic irony, yet somehow apt, that even after his death, Ste was at odds with the system and the authorities. He was always pushing for change and improvement, and it would have cheered him up to think that lessons had been learned after the handling of my futile 999 call.

The assistant coroner for North Manchester, Julie Robertson, decided that the delay did not have a bearing on his death and a verdict of suicide was recorded. I left the hearing feeling as desperate and lost as I was beforehand. Like the funeral, it brought me no solace at all.

Day after day, I wandered, lost and lonely, through a world I no longer recognised. Once again, I was besieged by those childhood feelings that I did not belong. Sucked into a vortex of pain, I continued to lose weight, I drank too much, and I cut myself off from my friends and family. Isolated and afraid, I dreaded each day, but I dreaded the night-time even more.

Haunted by flashbacks and nightmares, I had recurring dreams of the attacks, of Chowdhury and his vulture-like eyes as he raped me over and over without mercy. When it came to the part where he made me clean myself in the bathroom, the water sloshed around my feet and the levels rose and rose until I was struggling to stay afloat.

Each time, I woke from my nightmare at the point the water touched my nose, not knowing if I had been able to swim to safety or I had drowned in his bathroom. Other nights, I dreamed of Ste and his beautiful proposal on the chilly North Wales beach.

'Yes!' I beamed, my face radiant in my dream. 'Yes, I'll marry you.'

It felt so real. I could even taste the salt spray on my tongue. But as Ste was opening the ring box, he was swept away by a giant wave and carried far off into the sea. I searched for him all day, until darkness fell and I refused to leave the beach. When his body was washed up the following morning, there was a noose around his neck and I woke up screaming.

'No, Ste! No!' I yelled. 'Why did you leave us?'

In those dark and endless hours, I had thoughts of ending my own life. But the images of my three children, who needed me now more than ever, kept me alive.

I knew I could never, would never, follow Ste. Yet living was so much harder than dying.

29

IN FEBRUARY 2022, I was contacted by Malcolm Newsam CBE and Gary Ridgway, who were in charge of the Oldham child sexual exploitation inquiry. This was the review that had been requested back in 2019 by Oldham Council and the Oldham Safeguarding Partnership, and commissioned by the Greater Manchester Combined Authority (GMCA). Mr Newsam was the former commissioner for social care in Rotherham, and Mr Ridgway was a former detective superintendent of Cambridgeshire Police. I learned that, in the previous year, a social worker had decided on my behalf that I was not mentally strong enough to give evidence to the inquiry. Perhaps it was this, yet another example of someone making a decision on my behalf and not in my best interests, which sharpened my response.

'Yes, I'll give evidence,' I told them. 'I'll be the one to decide how I feel, not the social workers.'

After several meetings, I was informed that my evidence would be included in a review to be published later that year, in which I would be anonymised and known as 'Sophie'.

In June 2022, as the review was made public, a copy dropped through my letterbox. Despite the positive approach of the investigators, I did not hold out much hope. I had been failed time and time again by the system and I had no reason to think this review would be any different.

The investigation had quite a narrow scope – from 2011-2014 – and looked at issues such as grooming in children's homes, the risks posed by shisha establishments, the use of taxi services in child sexual exploitation, the development of the 'Messenger Service', which was designed to protect children at risk of harm, and the occasions where known offenders had previously been employed within the council and had been inadequately investigated. In total, 11 survivors had been interviewed, and Chapter 8 was dedicated solely to my complaint, which was outside the time frame of the other issues. My heart rate quickened as I leafed through the 200-page bundle to my chapter.

'In respect of Oldham Council,' the report said. 'There were significant opportunities missed by children's social care to intervene and put in place appropriate arrangements to protect Sophie.

'There were two specific incidents where there was evidence that Sophie was at risk of significant harm; this should have led to a multi-agency strategy meeting and joint police and children's social care investigation. Subsequently, the chair of the Home Affairs Select Committee raised Sophie's case with Oldham Council and asked the council to let them know what steps had been taken to protect her.

'The council's response was inadequate... A competent review of Sophie's file would have revealed the numerous warning signs and also that the council and Greater Manchester Police had failed to follow their own procedures in respect of protecting Sophie, who was only 12 years old at the time, from the risk of serious harm. There were at least two occasions when multi-agency child protection procedures should have been initiated and, if they had been, Sophie may have been protected from the predatory males who ended up abusing her.'

I could barely believe my eyes. I knew all of this, of course. But it was another matter entirely to see it written down in black and white. The report continued:

'In respect of Greater Manchester Police, there were serious failures in its investigation of [Paul Waites] who in 2006 groomed and sexually exploited Sophie when she was 12 years old.

'In our opinion there was sufficient information available to the officers investigating the series of rapes against Sophie in October 2006 to identify [Waites] as a potential threat to Sophie. We regard this as a missed opportunity. If further action had been taken it could in all probability have led to the earlier apprehension and conviction of [Waites].

'There were several failures in the subsequent investigation of the multiple rapes of Sophie by several offenders in 2006. We believe there were a number of proportionate and reasonable lines of enquiry available based on Sophie's interviews to investigate these offences. While the investigating officer asserts that appropriate enquiries were conducted into the sexual assault of Sophie in a churchyard and her rape by two men she alleged to have met at the police station, we have seen no evidence to enable us to provide assurance that this was done.

'Furthermore, Sophie also alleged that when she reported the initial crime of sexual assault at the police station, she was told to come back with an adult when she was not drunk. If she had received, at that point, the appropriate response required to protect her, she would have been spared the ordeal she was subsequently subjected to.

'The response to Sophie by staff and police officers on duty at Oldham Police Station was not considered at the time and in our view, it should have been. Although this incident and the multiple rapes were reported to Oldham Council, neither Oldham Council nor Greater Manchester Police initiated a strategy discussion that, as we have said earlier, would have ensured these shortcomings were identified and an adequate protection plan put in place around Sophie.

'In our view Greater Manchester Police has compounded these failures by presenting a less than candid approach to an enquiry by the chair of the Home Affairs Select Committee and responses to complaints made by Sophie and her husband by the Greater Manchester Police professional standards branch. In May 2007, a man [Shakil Chowdhury] was found guilty and sentenced to six years' imprisonment for the rape of Sophie. During his trial, as part of his mitigation, he named two other men involved with the rapes of Sophie.

'This information was not followed up by Greater Manchester Police at the time. We consider this to be a further serious failure and [it] was not considered by the professional standards investigations in 2013 or 2018... We have set out the several serious failures in the 2006 investigation, and it is disappointing that the professional standards branch investigation did not acknowledge these at the time to both Sophie and her husband, nor the disclosures made by [Chowdhury] in his trial. This is all the more troubling as we know that Greater Manchester Police had commenced an internal investigatory review that concluded on 6 March 2014. This identified the serious weaknesses in the original investigation and led to a major police investigation known as Operation Solent.

'It is therefore clear that in early 2014 Greater Manchester Police was aware of the many serious weaknesses in the original investigation. These weaknesses were not acknowledged to Sophie or her husband at the time.

'In May 2018, the professional standards branch within Greater Manchester Police undertook a further review of complaints submitted by Sophie. We are concerned that the conclusions of both of the internal professional standards branch reviews are significantly at variance with the conclusions of Operation Solent, which candidly recognised the failures within the 2006 investigation and our own assessment of the investigation. Insufficient regard has been given to the failure of Greater Manchester Police and its partners to respond appropriately to the threat of harm presented to Sophie and a failure to follow the child protection procedures in place at the time. This lack of candour in response to Sophie's legitimate complaints is deeply concerning.'

With each word, the burden on my shoulders grew lighter

and lighter, as in sheer disbelief, the tears streamed down my cheeks and on to the pages. At last, someone was listening. At last, the truth was out there.

'Oh Ste,' I said softly. 'I only wish you were here to read this with me.'

The litany of failures went on and on. The review confirmed Paul Waites had previously been jailed for possessing indecent images of children. And in 2020, he had received a life sentence for raping another child.

The review criticised Oldham Council and Greater Manchester Police for their response to the threat he posed. I found out my parents had contacted Paul Waites themselves when I was missing. The police had also called him and left him a voicemail when I was missing on the night of the gang rapes. But he was not investigated further. The review said:

'Our judgement is that there were serious failings in the investigation of the crimes reported by Sophie.'

Incredibly, the assault in the churchyard and the attacks in the car with the two men outside the police station were not even recorded as crimes. I flashed back to my despair over why the police had not been able to track down my abusers, and why there was no CCTV or eyewitnesses.

The answer was blindingly obvious: the attacks, violations of the worst kind, were not even considered a crime. I had thought I might die in that car. I had been so afraid that I had wet myself. I'd been raped and sexually assaulted and treated like dirt. Yet the police did not even think that merited investigation. It was a sucker punch, right to the stomach. I felt like they had been laughing at me, all along.

Oh, she's just a slut, she brings it on herself. She makes a mess of everything.

The report was heavily critical of my social workers, saying:

'Sophie maintained her view that she wanted to come into care and shared with the worker that she "had been talking to older men on the internet".

'The outreach worker recorded that she discussed the dangers of this with Sophie during this session and added that "Sophie appears to try to gain attention and shock others by what she says"…Sophie recounted to her social worker that recently "she had tried to meet an older man on a chatline"…Sophie reported to the outreach worker that that she had "been in contact with a man of 19 from the internet". She also said that she had met him on one occasion in Sainsbury's car park.

'Once again, the outreach worker discussed the dangers of this with Sophie. Sophie stated she had no sexual partners… The outreach worker concluded the record by stating: "She seems to enjoy telling me things to impress or shock me. It is very difficult to know when Sophie is telling the truth or inventing stories".'

The review also revealed the sexual health clinic I had attended had made a referral to social services' who had agreed to contact police. When I failed to attend an appointment, my referral was closed, and police were not informed. My outreach worker said I was: 'prone to fantasise'.

After the gang rapes, I was referred to children's social care in November 2006 and the review reported that the duty worker wrote:

'this child appears to be putting herself at risk'.

The naivety of the comment, the decades-old prejudice, took my breath away. *Putting herself at risk.* As if it was my fault, as if, aged 12, I was the one to blame. And still, the mistakes kept on coming.

The review confirmed that one of the men arrested for the gang rapes was an illegal immigrant who, after his release on bail, had predictably vanished. During his trial, as part of his mitigation, Shakil Chowdhury had named two other men involved with the rapes. This information was not followed up by Greater Manchester Police.

The review revealed that in July 2007, when I was 13, one of my relatives had telephoned children's social care to discuss their concerns about my welfare. The relative firstly mentioned the court case in respect of the rapes and cited that 'Sophie' was allowed to smoke, drink and 'date much older men'.

The relative was informed that children's social care had no current involvement and was advised to let the court case finish and only then discuss her concerns with my parents. If she remained concerned after that time, she was advised that she could again contact children's social care. The review claimed:

'This is very poor advice given Sophie's severe vulnerability, and her recent history of exploitation.'

I read that, in 2009, one of the suspects of the gang rape attacks was convicted of the attempted murder of his wife. An organisational review by Greater Manchester Police in 2014 concluded that, had the forensic enquiries been completed in 2006, the offender may have been identified, and this may have prevented his assault on his wife in 2009.

In conclusion, the review stated:

'We believe that the interventions of both the council and Greater Manchester Police fell far short of what was required to protect Sophie at the time and these failures have been compounded by the denials that have subsequently been issued to Sophie and feed a view that both agencies were more concerned about covering up their failures than acknowledging the harm that had been done to a vulnerable young person.

'We recommend that both Greater Manchester Police and Oldham Council publicly acknowledge these serious failures and apologise to Sophie.'

There was vindication on every page. I had waited 16 years for someone to admit that I had been failed. Now the mistakes were being brutally exposed, one by one, popping up like boils. At first, I felt giddy with relief and euphoria. I was not a nuisance, I was not a liar, and I was not a fantasist. I was a victim of crime, with legitimate and serious complaints, and the authorities had let me down.

I had already known much of what was contained in the reports. But to see it written and accepted by others, in a formalised review, was mind-blowing. As the hours passed, my euphoria slowly drained away and I was overtaken by a growing fizz of anger and frustration. How had they got away with this for so long? Why had these failings been covered up and ignored, year after year after year? And in the meantime, how many other young girls, like me, had slipped through the net, unnoticed, unimportant, unloved?

It was not enough to simply apologise and move on. I needed to know why the mistakes had happened, and what sanctions, if any, had been handed out to the people who had made them.

Most importantly, I wanted a reassurance that these errors would not happen again. The police and social services had dedicated years to trying to cover up and deny the grotesque mistakes they had made in my care, instead of owning up and making changes. Re-reading the review, I scribbled down notes and highlighted what I felt was significant.

'This has to be a turning point,' I told myself. 'This has to make a difference.'

The report was at once highly compelling and important, yet at the same time woefully impotent. Because although the criticism was unequivocal, the investigators had no power to ensure punishments or change for the future.

That night, with my anger drizzling away, my thoughts turned again to Ste. He'd have been so proud to see his hard work come to fruition at last.

Maybe this review would give me the strength to pick up where we had both left off when our relationship started to fall apart. It broke my heart that Ste was not here to see his own success, and yet it made me all the more determined to see this through myself.

In that moment, I set aside my anger and grief, and I thought of him in a rare moment of love. In the darkness, I heard him whisper, so close his head could have been on the pillow next to me:

Keep fighting, Sam. You're not on your own.

30

THE REVIEW, and its damning condemnation of the police and social services, was certainly a boost for my mental health. But like waking from a coma, my recovery was so gradual that some days I barely noticed any improvement. Sometimes, on a birthday, an anniversary, or with a simple reminder of my lost family, I slumped back to feeling worse than before. But as the fog of grief and pain slowly eased, I began to think more seriously about continuing the campaign.

Ste had launched our fight with the right intentions, out of a sense of love for me and a wider desire for justice for all victims of child grooming. But as his health deteriorated and he became fixated firstly on the campaign and later on me, those pure intentions became warped and muddied. He lost sight – we both did – of what mattered. Nothing could change the hurt or wipe away my trauma. But I recognised that the campaign itself had been a positive force and I nurtured a growing desire to ensure other children were kept safe and the authorities were held to account.

In his goodbye email, Ste had shared a list of links to his campaign work, including the pin codes and passwords for each file. Immersing myself in past memories, I heard his voice once again, and rediscovered that old spark and that determination to put right a wrong.

Sam! Look at this letter! We're going to Parliament!

I owed it to all other victims of grooming, and most of all to myself, to continue the fight. Despite our differences at the end, Ste knew me better than anyone else ever had. He had left the files and the passwords ready, because he knew that one day I would take up the mantle. The fight needed me, and I needed the fight. For, though I had lost absolutely everything, I had so much more to give. A few years earlier, I'd joined a support group run by The Maggie Oliver Foundation, a charity aimed at supporting survivors of childhood sexual abuse and exploitation.

At the meetings, I was introduced to other survivors and I hit it off immediately with several of the other girls. Talking to them was like listening to myself. We shared the same anxieties and those instantly recognisable feelings of blame and shame. Like me, they had at times been overcome by the belief they were worthless and did not deserve justice. Unlike me, many had found peace.

'You will find it too,' they promised. 'It just takes time.'

Soon, I had made new friendships within the group, and Maria and Debbie were always there for me. Though the pain and shock from Ste's death remained, my mind was becoming clearer, with the support of my friends. I was searching for answers, for reasons why he had taken his life, why I had been groomed as a child, why I had been failed, time after time, by the very authorities who were supposed to keep me safe. The questions ricocheted around my head, smashing from one side of my skull to the next. My mind was so full all of the time. Each day felt like I was running on a hamster wheel and I could never slow down long enough to jump off.

'I need a break from my own thoughts,' I told Debbie. 'But I don't know how to switch off.'

I had never been especially religious. But I had a Muslim friend, Tahir Mushtaq, who had been really kind to me after Ste had died and had supported me through the darkness of the past few months. I knew he took great comfort from his faith.

'Life is a test,' Tahir told me. 'Humans are put on earth to be tested by Allah through their choice and their actions. And those tested hardest are Allah's soldiers who he loves the most.'

His words struck a chord within me, because my entire life had felt like a challenge. And seen through the eyes of Islam, it all made sense. I was being tested on earth because Allah loved me and he would reward me in the afterlife. I made the decision to convert to Islam. I did not find answers to why I had suffered so much. But I found a sort of peace, and a promise that I was not alone.

After the review was made public, I wrote to GMP to request that an outside police force investigate their failings in my case. I could not help rewinding back to those early days of the campaign, when Ste had fired off letters, phone calls and emails to everyone he could think of. We had been filled with such excitement back then, believing we could change the world. And in a small way, perhaps we had. The chief constable replied swiftly, but predictably, refusing my request and instead explaining that they were working with Operation Hydrant, a national team outside of GMP, overseeing and co-ordinating non-recent child sex abuse investigations, providing reviews, support and advice to police. Operation Hydrant, he promised, would be looking into my case.

'I won't hold my breath,' I said, as I folded his letter away.

Almost three years on, I am still waiting to hear from them and I imagine I never will. In line with the conclusions of the Oldham review, I was invited to attend a meeting with the police in the centre of Manchester, so that they could make an apology to me in person. I have no doubt that their apologies were heartfelt, but that sincerity didn't help me understand how they would act differently, going forward.

Oldham Council made no effort at all, they simply sent me a brief apology in the post – and probably only because they were told to. They didn't even bother following it up with a phone call. And while the apologies were a step forward, neither meant a thing without positive change.

31

WITH THE spark lit, I was ready for battle and I arranged a meeting with my MP and with local councillors. After discussions, we agreed the best way forward would be to push for a full public inquiry. The local review, while it addressed important issues, did not go far enough and did not have the power needed to hold to account the authorities and their failures.

A public inquiry would include a series of official investigations, established by a UK or devolved government minister and conducted by an independent body. A statutory inquiry would have special powers to compel testimony and the release of other forms of evidence. I called a meeting of local survivors, with supportive local councillors attending, too.

'We need a public inquiry,' I said. 'It's not enough for different agencies to just apologise when their mistakes are exposed.'

In the meantime, I planned to pressurise Oldham Council into holding another local inquiry, with a wider remit than the first one. Though the 2022 review had been brilliant in many ways, it had looked at only 11 cases over a narrow time period from 2011-2014. My own complaint had been outside of that time frame, but had been included largely, I think, because of Ste's persistence. But there were countless child grooming victims, spanning several decades. I wanted all voices to be heard. It was a huge challenge, and I felt like I was standing at the foot of a mountain – in flip-flops! But, I reminded myself, I had been through much worse than this. I had survived grooming, sexual assaults and rapes. I had just about survived the implosion of my family. Seen in those terms, securing an inquiry really wouldn't be that much of a problem.

Over Facebook, I started chatting to a man named Amir, who lived nearby and we quickly became friends. Like me, he loved films and enjoyed long walks. He knew a little about what I had been through, and he seemed supportive and kind.

'Let's meet up,' he suggested. 'Do you fancy a walk?'

I was only looking for friendship, but we quickly fell into a relationship, which just as quickly became very intense. I let myself be carried along on the crest of something new and exciting, believing a new partner would help me to move on from Ste and plug the huge holes in my life. Amir was well travelled and suggested we take a trip around Europe.

'It would do you good to get away,' he said.

I nodded in agreement. I was willing to try anything to help me adjust to this strange and frightening world without my family in it. So someone offering to take me across Europe was exactly what I needed – so much so that I failed to really question whether we should even have been together in the first place.

Over a period of several months, I drove across France and Belgium and into Holland. I'd dreaded driving into the centre of Manchester in the past, so this felt like a leap out of my comfort zone. But then I told myself that was surely a good thing, because it was exactly what I needed. I enjoyed seeing unfamiliar places and trying new foods, but deep down, I knew I was making a mistake with Amir. And back at home, we argued a lot. He did not like me posting selfies on social media. He complained about the way I dressed, and he didn't like my make-up. I was only allowed to spend my own money with his supervision. This time, the warning signs flashed like bright beacons before me.

'I've been through all this before,' I told him. 'I'm not being controlled by another man ever again. I've had enough.'

But when I tried to end it, Amir quickly became nasty. He sent messages threatening me and telling me I was fat and ugly. In one horrendous exchange, he referred to the attacks from 2006, saying:

'You went with eight men.'

'I don't do use[d] items.'

'You're the ugliest.'

I was heartbroken that someone I had trusted and confided in could be so cruel. Though I went to the police to report his behaviour, I didn't feel I could handle yet another court case and yet another inevitable let-down. I was done with the justice system.

I tried to put the whole thing behind me, but his words

lingered, like an illness, in my mind. Was I so insignificant, so contemptible, that it was acceptable to use the rapes against me? What was it about me that made men think they could abuse me in any way they liked? I felt myself sinking into another quicksand depression. But Debbie, who had been keeping an eye on me, stepped in to help.

'Come and stay with me,' she offered. 'You need people around you. He's not even worth thinking about. He's just another abuser. You'll soon get over him.' I was so grateful to her.

After a while, I moved to a new house, which, the council warned, was an absolute tip.

'You'll have your work cut out,' said the housing officer, as she handed over the keys.

'Don't worry about that,' I grinned. 'I love a bit of DIY. I can't wait to get started.'

I spent the next few months cathartically stripping walls, filling holes and skimming surfaces. I decorated every room and bought new carpets and furniture. My home became a little haven, just as it had been when I was small. And slowly, I thought less about relationships and more about my campaign.

As 2024 came around, I set myself a goal of a new review for Oldham.

32

UNSURE WHETHER I was doing the right thing, I pulled my best coat and boots out of the wardrobe, ready to attend my first council meeting. My plan was to turn up to every single meeting, until somebody listened to me.

On the bus journey there, I had the usual flutters of panic when the old landmarks loomed into view: the Sainsbury's car park, the library, the churchyard. But now, I closed my eyes and breathed deeply, and reminded myself I was not a child, and the perpetrators could no longer hurt me.

These were just inanimate buildings, and I had no need to fear their links with the past. There were many children out there who were going through abuse right now, many who were experiencing that same fear and dread, and this was why the new review was all the more vital.

I felt quite excited as I took my seat in the public gallery, but I was nervous too. An irrational part of me worried that one of the councillors might pick me out and say:

'Samantha Walker-Roberts! You have no right to be here! You have no voice!'

Even now, after the vindication by the review, I worried I was making a fuss about nothing. I reassured myself I had as much right to be here as anyone else, and besides, the council members wouldn't even recognise me. I smoothed out my nerves, but after a few minutes of listening to the items on the agenda, I felt my mind wandering. I'd had no idea how boring council meetings were! They seemed to spend ages discussing their budget deficit. And then longer still talking about potholes and how there was no money to fill them. And so, when my item was finally mentioned at the very end, it was quickly slapped down.

'There are no funds for a review,' said one of the councillors. 'None at all.'

But I was not about to give up. I returned the next month, and the next. I sat through mind-numbing debates about sewage and landfill and, the old favourite, the lack of funds. Two or three councillors were firmly on my side, and Brian Hobin, an independent, was the most helpful. But more were needed to swing the vote in my favour. To strengthen our argument, I contacted Holly Archer, herself a survivor of child sexual exploitation (CSE), who had secured a review in Telford, similar to the one I was hoping for in Oldham.

'Let's meet up,' she suggested. 'I'm happy to help wherever I can.'

I drove to Telford and Holly and I clicked together from that first moment. Our circumstances were different, but the trauma was sadly the same. It was useful to pick up tips on what the Telford inquiry had done well and on what they had missed. It was nice, too, to have made a good friend.

'Stay in touch,' she smiled, and I knew we would.

Back in Oldham, I continued attending council meetings, applying as much pressure as I could.

'There's no money, Sam,' I was told, over and over again.

In September 2024, prior to another meeting, I met with Brian Hobin, who seemed unusually optimistic. In the meeting itself, I hardly dared to hope, and I held my breath as the motion was put to the vote. My heart hammered so loudly in my chest I was worried I might not hear the chairman announcing the decision.

'The vote is in favour. The inquiry will go ahead,' he said, as though it had never been in any doubt.

Dropping my head into my hands, I blinked back tears. Rolling up my sleeve, I read the words of the campaign on my tattoo, and I smiled.

You have not defeated me.

It had been worth it, after all. Oldham Council later voted unanimously to request a Government-led review into CSE. I held little hope of the Government agreeing to this, and it was quietly rejected by Jess Phillips, the Minister for Safeguarding. It felt to me that the matter did not seem to concern anyone outside Oldham.

The world's media did not appear especially interested in the plight of survivors or in our efforts to expose what had gone wrong. But waking one morning in January 2025, my phone lit up with messages and missed calls. Just when I thought life couldn't throw any more twists and turns, I read that Elon Musk, the US billionaire, had waded feet first into the argument on grooming gangs. And Oldham was right at the centre of the debate. On X, Mr Musk wrote:

'In the UK, serious crimes such as rape require the Crown Prosecution Service's approval for the police to charge suspects. Who was the head of the CPS when rape gangs were allowed to exploit young girls without facing justice? Keir Starmer, 2008-2013.'

He also criticised Jess Phillips, claiming she 'deserves to be in prison', for refusing to hold a public inquiry. I was bemused, but pleased that someone was at least taking notice. I didn't even realise Elon Musk knew where Oldham was!

His comments were like an atom bomb and the inquiry, or lack of it, was suddenly on every news channel and in every headline. Politicians argued and debated, each side keen to score points. Kemi Badenoch, the leader of the opposition, argued that survivors had waited many years for justice, and that a public inquiry in 2025 was the only way.

Labour politicians argued that the Conservative Party had done nothing throughout their years in power to bring about an inquiry. Mostly, they all felt Elon Musk had no business involving himself in British politics, but I didn't mind one bit. An issue that people had been ignoring was now top of the news agenda and everyone was talking about it. That surely had to be a good thing.

That same week, I was invited, along with two other survivors, including Holly Archer, to meet with Jess Phillips. I already knew she was in favour of a local inquiry only.

'I disagree,' I told her bluntly. 'We've had a local inquiry and nothing has changed. There was a lot of finger-pointing, but what good is that? I received an apology from the council and the police, but that won't change anything. I don't want words. I want action.'

The following week, I was invited to meet with Kemi Badenoch at Westminster. An Uber arrived at my door to collect me before it was even light and the driver took me the whole way to London. Kemi reiterated that she was in favour of a Government-led inquiry, leaving no stone unturned. But a few days later, the Government announced they were not prepared to back it. It was a setback, but it was expected, I was well used to these by now. And it was promising to receive another invite to see Jess Phillips, this time in Manchester.

We met up at the Pankhurst Museum, the former home of Emmeline Pankhurst, who had fought for women to get the vote. Walking around the museum, reading the stories of the Pankhurst family, was at once inspiring and depressing. This was clearly a place where great change had been planned and realised. Society had made many impressive strides forward since Emmeline's death in 1928 and yet in other ways, we were stumbling backwards. Would those great suffragettes have been proud of Great Britain 2025, where vulnerable children are exploited and groomed by predators and the authorities who fail to help them get justice are simply allowed to get away with it? This meeting with Jess was more productive than the last and she assured me that the new Oldham inquiry would have a broader scope than the first one.

'Trust me,' she said.

This was something I always struggled to do. But I conceded I really had no other choice.

One weekend in June, I was idly flicking through my phone when a flashing headline caught my eye: 'Starmer makes U-turn over grooming gangs inquiry'!

I could hardly believe it. I read the article, which confirmed a full national statutory inquiry into grooming gangs, meaning that witnesses would be compelled to provide evidence and answer questions. It was such a big step forward. Running alongside the local inquiry, this was the biggest step towards change that we'd ever had. It was the best news I could have hoped for.

Meanwhile, we were still waiting for the start of the Oldham inquiry, which had already, worryingly, been postponed, and I was concerned our message was becoming lost in local politics. So, I started working with John Piekos, a former police officer, with a view to setting up our own survivors' group.

One way or another, I was determined to have my voice heard. Whilst awaiting a start date for both inquiries, I've kept busy compiling issues of importance. From a personal standpoint, I would like to know why the two suspects identified by Shakil Chowdhury were never arrested at the time of the trial and, equally importantly, why they haven't been arrested since. It is not too late to take these rapists off the streets to face justice.

There is also a third suspect, whose wife gave his name to police, who was never arrested. Again, it is not too late for him to be charged.

From a wider perspective, I would like to see education and information to remove the link between race and grooming. A Home Office report in 2020 said there was not enough evidence to conclude that child sexual abuse gangs were disproportionately made up of Asian offenders. And more recently, in February 2025, eight members of a predominantly white male grooming gang were jailed for child sex offences. The link with race simply encourages far-right racism and it is not constructive.

Going forward, to help prevent other children being ensnared by grooming gangs, I have so many ideas and areas of interest. I would like to see anonymous suggestion boxes for children in every town, including in mosques, churches, synagogues, schools, libraries and leisure centres. I would also advocate early education surrounding exploitation and grooming, so that young children grow up knowing the danger signs, how to avoid them and how to report them safely.

We need clear and evidenced cross-agency communication, so at-risk children do not slip through the safety nets as I did. Issues that did not affect me, such as HIV testing and overseas trafficking, need to be examined and overhauled. It would be helpful for potential links in the grooming chain, such as taxi firms, taxi drivers and takeaway owners, to work more closely with child protection agencies.

More than anything, all agencies, such as social services and the polic, must be transparent and accountable and internet providers and social media sites must take more responsibility for content. I am so excited to see some of these ideas put into practice and I know that our children will be safer as a result.

Away from the inquiry, Paul Waites is due for parole in May 2026 and there is a possibility he may be released. I have been asked to write to the parole board to explain why that must never happen. Waites frightens me more than any of the gang members who raped me in 2006. He is conniving and manipulative in a way that sends shivers through me, and I believe he will always be a danger to children. Hopefully, he will remain in prison for a long time to come.

I'm planning to leave Oldham this year, for as much as I have learned to ignore the triggers around me, I would like a fresh start. Every day, I think about the rapes. Leaving my house, I still scan the street for strangers.

My attackers are out there and I cannot fully move on until they face justice. I love my town, but feel I would love it more from afar. Living on my own, I am thankful for Debbie and the friends who support me. Maria is the best mum-in-law I could wish for and she and I have become closer than ever since losing Ste. Long-term relationships are not easy for me, and perhaps they will always be that way.

The trauma from the rapes seems to poke its ugly head into every occasion, even the most intimate. In the future, I hope I can sit down with my three children and explain what went wrong and why. I would like them to know I always loved them very much. The problem was, I didn't love myself enough. I hope, without me, my children can have a better life and that one day we can all be reunited.

I cannot change my own journey. But I am committed now to changing the system for other children and turning my trauma into triumph. In February 2025, my local paper ran a story claiming people are ashamed to be from Oldham because of the way the grooming gang scandals have been mishandled and because of the conflict between our political leaders. I hope a new inquiry can change this and bring the pride back to our town. I also hope other towns and cities around the UK will take hope from our campaign. Just recently, I read that Karen Downes, the bereaved mother of a grooming gang victim, is asking for a review in Blackpool. Every town has something to learn.

Looking back, I can appreciate how far we have come. But there is also such a long way to go. Our fight is about the power of persistence, the sheer strength of the human spirit and the importance of holding the justice system to account. If the attacks ripped me to pieces, then this crusade is slowly putting me back together, rebuilding what was broken and making me stronger than before.

You have not defeated me.

And you never will.

Acknowledgements

THANKS TO Debbie for saving me and taking care of me at my worst. To all survivors out there, I hope this gives you the courage and fire deep down within to keep fighting and to get to the truth.

Other bestselling Mirror Books

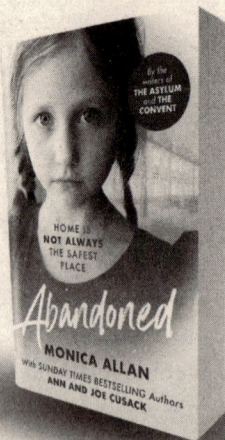

Abandoned

Monica Allan

With Ann Cusack

Monica was just five years old when her mother tried to kill her by forcing her head under running bathroom taps. She had already tried to strangle her as a baby

Escaping into foster care, Monica would go on to experience horrific physical and sexual abuse at the hands of those she hoped would protect her. She tried to find a new life and raise a loving family of her own. But living with the devastating secrets that had been buried for so long proved too painful.

Enough was enough. To live again, she knew she had to confront the demons of her past.

written by Ann Cusack

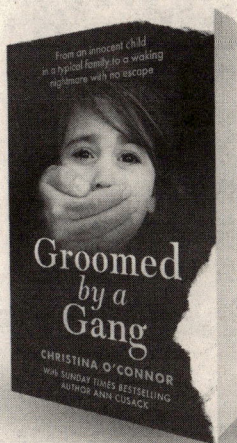

Groomed by a Gang
Christina O'Connor

With Ann Cusack

'I can't change the path I took – or the one I was forced to take – but I can tell my story to try and make sure that my child, and all children, grow up knowing about the evils of grooming'

Christina O'Connor was a normal girl in a normal family – yet she would make national headlines as the main prosecution witness in a national grooming scandal that saw gang members jailed for a total of 257 years. Eleven men were convicted of multiple offences against her, including 22 counts of rape.

Now she bravely wants to tell her harrowing story to prevent others from suffering the same fate.

MIRROR BOOKS

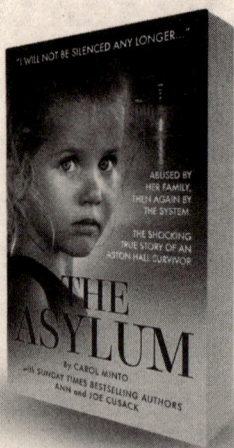

The Asylum

Carol Minto

With Ann Cusack

For 46 years, Carol Minto has quietly gone about her life, carrying with her the most extraordinary and heartbreaking secrets.

Born into poverty and with mostly absent parents, Carol helped to raise her nine siblings. But when she was just 11 years old, her older brother began to sexually abuse her. After four years, Carol managed to escape – and ran away from home.

In *The Asylum* Carol tells the full story of how she overcame unimaginable suffering, to find the happiness and solace she has today as a mother and grandmother.

mB

MIRROR BOOKS

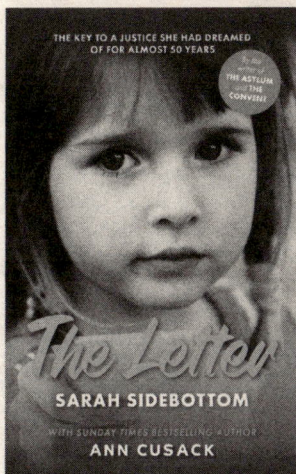

THE KEY TO A JUSTICE SHE HAD DREAMED
OF FOR ALMOST 50 YEARS

The Letter

SARAH SIDEBOTTOM

WITH SUNDAY TIMES BESTSELLING AUTHOR

ANN CUSACK

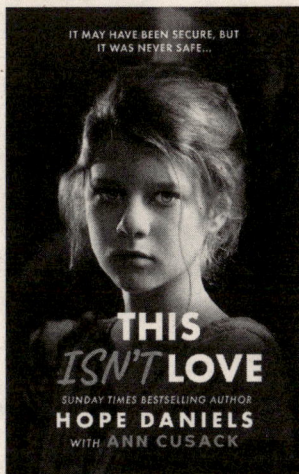

IT MAY HAVE BEEN SECURE, BUT
IT WAS NEVER SAFE...

THIS
ISN'T LOVE

SUNDAY TIMES BESTSELLING AUTHOR

HOPE DANIELS
with **ANN CUSACK**

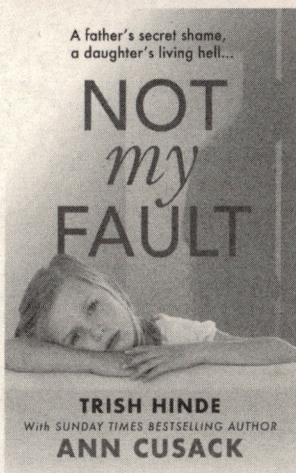

A father's secret shame,
a daughter's living hell...

NOT
my
FAULT

TRISH HINDE
With SUNDAY TIMES BESTSELLING AUTHOR
ANN CUSACK

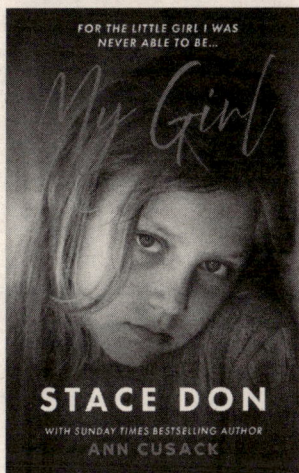

FOR THE LITTLE GIRL I WAS
NEVER ABLE TO BE...

My Girl

STACE DON

WITH SUNDAY TIMES BESTSELLING AUTHOR
ANN CUSACK